CANADA'S NATIONAL PARKS

**Text by
R. D. Lawrence**

*Photography by
William Curwen and Nick Meers*

**Collins
Toronto**

CONTENTS

FOREWORD

The author of the text of this book, Ronald Lawrence, has visited most of Canada's national parks many times. He writes of them with sure knowledge and deep appreciation. His text and the magnificent photographs specially commissioned by the publishers are a compelling invitation to enjoy the natural heritage of our beautiful country. There is at least one national park in each province and territory; but this national network is far from completed. Parks Canada, the agency responsible for national parks, has identified 48 distinct natural regions of Canada. Its objective is to have at least one national park in each natural region. Less than half of the 48 regions are represented in the present system.

The national parks preserve for public enjoyment representative areas of the natural wilderness and great beauty of our land. The Parliament of Canada has dedicated these lands, "to the people of Canada for their benefit, education and enjoyment . . . to be made use of so as to leave them unimpaired for the enjoyment of future generations."

Our national parks are an insurance policy, a way of making sure that Canadians, and the people who visit our country always have places in which to admire the rich variety of landscape, animals and plants that make up Canada. National parks are reference points for the protection of our environment, reminders of the original face of the land. They are also places to inspire feelings of awe and reverence, places where we can explore not only the land, but ourselves.

The first national park was established in 1885 at Banff – in what was then called the North West Territories. The discovery of mineral hot springs, "which promise to be of great sanitary advantage to the public," prompted the Government of Canada to set aside ten square miles for future park use.

In 1981, more than 21 million people visited the national parks. Maintaining a balance between preservation and wise use has always been the challenge of managing the national parks. In recent times, economic considerations have added to that challenge. The economic impact of employment created within and by the parks, the expenditures for goods and services, and the tourism revenue generated by the national parks is estimated at $600 million and 29000 jobs per year; but the greatest contribution of the national parks is beyond price and could never be measured. Undimmed by time, Banff is the shining jewel in a nationwide system of national parks and historic sites that extends into every province and both territories. Speaking in the House of Commons during the 1887 debate to establish Rocky Mountains National Park, Sir Donald Smith, who drove the last spike in the first transcontinental railway, said, "Anyone who has gone to Banff . . . and not felt himself elevated and proud that all this is a part of the Dominion, cannot be a Canadian." In each of Canada's national parks, the visitor who seeks will find a reason to feel elevated and proud.

Jim Shearon,
Director, Information Services,
Parks Canada.

INTRODUCTION

In 1885, ten years before Alberta was created a province, Canada's first national park was established at Banff by our federal government. The Canadian Pacific·Railway had been completed that same year and at a time when this nation consisted of seven provinces and a vast wilderness, the whole of which was then designated as the Northwest Territories.

Today, 97 years later, all land south of latitude 60 (except for the northernmost tip of Labrador) has been taken over by ten provinces and the remainder – about 40 per cent of our nation – has been divided into the Yukon Territory and the Northwest Territories.

During that same span of time, 28 national parks have been added to a system that collectively encompasses about 130000 km². Banff, meanwhile – somewhat less than a century after its establishment – recorded nearly four million visitors in 1981, setting an all-time, all-parks record during a year when more than 21 million people passed through our national parks.

The fact that so many millions were attracted to our parks (a total of visitors almost equal to the population of Canada) is itself testimony to the success of the system; but of even greater significance, in my view, is that so many felt the need to leave other environments in order to commune, however briefly, with the natural lands that have been set aside for this purpose. As one who has been deeply committed to the wilderness for almost an entire lifetime, I find this encouraging, for I have long been aware of and sought to share the pleasure, the peace and the stimulus that are to be obtained from intimate contact with nature.

It would seem that before the 1960s, North Americans as a whole and Canadians in particular tended to take their environment for granted, aware of its vastness and availability, but too busy with their immediate affairs to get to know their land. Then came a change in social attitudes, the one that is reflected by the attendance records of Canada's national parks: as international confrontations became more numerous and dangerous, as the cost of living climbed higher and cities grew larger in response to growing populations, and as the pace became faster and more demanding, urban stress increased dramatically.

In 1960, five million people visited Canada's national parks; 21 years later the number had more than quadrupled. Even allowing for the rise in population that occurred in the interim and the creation of ten new national parks since 1968, the increase is dramatic and I believe it is due to more and more individuals searching for the kind of inner peace that is available only in natural settings.

Henry David Thoreau recognized this almost a century and a half ago when he wrote in his book, *Walden:* ". . . what I have been preparing to say is, that in Wildness is the preservation of the World. The cities import it at any price. Men plow and sail for it. From the forest and the wilderness come the tonic and barks which brace mankind."

By law, Canada's federal parklands are dedicated to people and for this reason the law also demands that they be conserved "unimpaired for future generations." This means that while park staff have a duty to welcome and encourage all visitors, they have an equal duty to ensure that the environment and all that it contains does not suffer at the hands of the careless or the destructive. As visitor pressure mounts, the job of conservation becomes increasingly difficult and would be downright impossible without the co-operation of those for whom the wild lands have been set aside. Our government plans an eventual total of 55 national parks, a goal that would give us the greatest system of its kind in the world and would also relieve some of the current pressures. But that is in the future.

Now, as I prepare to describe each of our national parks, I am most conscious of the responsibility that I have accepted, for although this book is clearly intended to encourage visitors to all 29 of them, it must also stress the importance of conserving in a healthy state these samples of our unique wilderness. It should be noted in this context that I have not used the word *preserving.*

It is largely believed that preservation and conservation amount to the same thing, but each term has a different meaning when applied to the environment. One may preserve an antique object, for example; properly cared for, it will last *unchanged* for countless ages. But nature cannot be preserved because it is always changing –

evolving. It is this ability to change at an exceptionally slow but progressive rate that must be conserved. This means that nature must not be tampered with by man; it must not be violated; it must not be forced to remain static by preservation. If we wish to keep our parks unimpaired, they must be allowed to change in their own ways and at their appointed times, as they have been doing since the dawn of creation.

To illustrate further: a forest fire set by a careless camper is a destructive force that must, if possible, be controlled by human agency. Such a fire is out of stride with the natural cycles of the land, the vegetation, the animals and the seasons. But a forest fire started by natural means should, from a conservation standpoint, be allowed to burn itself out; its timing is right because climatic, vegetative and land conditions are in its favor. Such fires create positive changes. In the pre-Columbus Americas, natural fires burned unmolested and helped to create the great forests and the profuse numbers of wildlife that existed then.

In similar vein, if one park visitor strips a piece of bark from a birch tree, no great harm will be done; though the tree will probably die – a pity, to be sure – the local species will survive. But if each of, say, one million visitors stripped bark from birches in a particular park, such vandalism would almost certainly lead to the extinction of the species in that region, a change that would be followed by other harmful alterations of the ecosystem. Such chain reactions arise because *nature is very fragile.*

It is difficult for the layman to understand that tall mountains, rushing rivers, or dense forests are fragile in any way; and lordly moose and great bears do not look a bit fragile to human eyes. Individually, perhaps they are not – at least from the standpoint of an awed park visitor. But all things, animate and inanimate alike, are utterly dependent upon their environments. They are collectively fragile. Alter the landscape in any unnatural way and a river may change its course, a forest may die, a moose may disappear and grizzlies may become extinct.

Few examples of human carelessness can better exemplify the fragility of nature than the history of the buffalo – or bison, as it is more correctly named – a story which, in 1963, led me to Wood Buffalo National Park so as to record its postscript. As I drove through North Dakota, Montana and Alberta, where vast herds of bison once dominated the landscape, I found it almost impossible to believe that such a legion of enormous, powerful animals had been almost totally wiped out in less than a century.

Estimates of the actual number of bison living in North America before European settlement range from a low of 30 million to a high of 70 million; but the actual number once present on a vast range that extended from the northern half of Mexico to the timberlands in Canada's north will never be known. The fact remains that ruthless slaughter and equally ruthless elimination of their range virtually wiped out all those millions of animals by 1905, when only a few hundred wild plains bison *(Bison bison)* were to be found on our entire continent. In the nick of time a few alarmed conservationists then banded together to save the remnants.

Earlier, in 1893, the Canadian government passed a law which gave complete protection to a handful of northern woods bison *(Bison bison athabascae)* that still existed in the Mackenzie River delta, a subspecies that had traditionally lived in Canada's woodlands but which, like their plains relatives, were also very close to extinction.

In 1906, our government again took measures to ensure the survival of bison when it purchased from an American rancher 709 plains animals for $200000. These were first shipped to a wilderness region that lies about 30 km east of Edmonton and was to become Elk Island National Park in 1913. The majority of the bison were later shipped to Buffalo Park near Wainwright, Alberta (a reserve that no longer exists), where they prospered, multiplying to 4609 animals by 1921 and continuing a rate of reproduction of about 25 per cent a year. Soon it became clear that unless something was done, the bison would over-graze their range. The first remedy was to shoot 2406 bison between 1922 and 1924. But as Wood Buffalo Park had also been created in 1922, authorities later decided to ship the animals to that reserve, which straddles the borders of Alberta and the Northwest Territories.

This complex "cattle drive" began in 1925, when the first bison were shipped by train, then by barge up the Athabasca River to the Slave River and eventual freedom in Wood Buffalo Park. When the transfer was completed in 1928, 6673 animals had been relocated.

This massive shipment of wild cattle created enormous transportation problems, but these were perhaps dwarfed by the howl of protest that came from conservationists in America and Canada when our government's plan was first made public. Opposition to the scheme was voiced because it was feared that the plains bison would interbreed with the woods bison and the latter subspecies become extinct. Canadian bureaucrats of the day would not listen.

History has proved the conservationists to have been almost right: *almost* in that the two different kinds of animals did, indeed, mate; but not quite - as far as the plains species was concerned - in that a small herd of purebreds had been left at Elk Island Park. The woods bison subspecies, however, was deemed to have become extinct.

But luck took a hand in the drama when in 1957 biologists of the Canadian Wildlife Service, Environment Canada, discovered a small, completely isolated herd of purebred woods bison in the Nyarling River area, in the northern section of Wood Buffalo Park. To ensure their survival, some of these were moved to the neighborhood of Fort Providence, Northwest Territories, and another group to Elk Island National Park, which now furnishes "seed stock" for periodic transfers of this endangered subspecies to other suitable ranges.

By the time I visited Wood Buffalo Park, survival of both pure strains of bison appeared assured; yet when I left Fort Smith, the nearest settlement to the park, I was quite unprepared for the heart-stopping sight of large (in today's terms) herds of buffalo grazing, standing, rolling and sometimes bellowing at each other in a section of magnificent and undisturbed wilderness. That the animals I was so close to were not purebred mattered not to me, for the spectacle was unforgettable.

Later, when I was allowed to take a quiet look at the purebred woods bison and was fortunate enough to see at close quarters two huge, dark-colored bulls, the difference between them and the crossbred animals was readily apparent.

It has been said for years that woods bison are darker in color and larger than their plains relatives but only in recent times - and because of the work of the Canadian Wildlife Service - have these things been confirmed scientifically. Now, after more than a century of vague references and specifically due to the herds of purebred plains *and* woods bison that are kept separated at Elk Island National Park, biologists such as Hal Reynolds of Edmonton have been able to study each breed and to weigh them accurately.

Bearing in mind that weight fluctuations in every species - including our own - vary considerably according to individuals, diet,

season and state of health, Reynolds now knows that the weight of some adult, ten-year-old woods bison bulls in good condition reaches 680 kilos and that adult females in the same class will probably weigh 545 kilos. Older bulls have been recorded at 816 kilos but because some of the really large woods bulls could not be fitted into the weighing chutes - which are now being modified - the maximum weight of one of these giant animals cannot yet be confirmed. Educated estimates suggest that an exceptionally large, old woods bison bull in full prime will weigh about 1360 kilos. By comparison, the plains animals show weights of 680 kilos for some adult bulls and 408 kilos for adult females, though exceptionally heavy individuals may well exist.

In the matter of coloration, while in their natural habitats the color of woods bison is definitely darker than that of plains bison, Reynolds points out that this, too, is variable. In some cases, woods bison living in more open country become lighter, but if they move back into a forest habitat, they revert to the dark shade. It is safe to say, however, that *Bison bison athabascae* is larger and of generally darker coat than *Bison bison*.

Thus, through the efforts of a small group of farsighted conservationists a century ago, the plains bison was saved from extinction; in our own times, despite early bureaucratic bumbling, modern biologists are working to remove the woods bison from the endangered list by stocking suitable ranges with animals bred at Elk Island National Park.

Wood Buffalo Park, occupying an area of 44807 km², is a magnificent example of Canada's northern boreal plains, a country where forests and enormous sections of open land intermingle, where there are marshes, lakes and rivers that offer shelter to 46 species of mammals and 227 species of birds. Perhaps the most important of these from a conservation standpoint is the whooping crane, the nesting site of which had been looked for in vain after the great birds were brought to the edge of extinction during the last quarter of the 19th century and the first quarter of the 20th.

By 1941, only 21 whooping cranes were known to exist in the wild. Nobody knew where they nested. In 1954, it was discovered that the five-foot tall cranes with the black and crimson top-knots nested in marshlands at the northern end of Wood Buffalo Park. Since then, biologists in Canada and in the U.S.A. have been working to ensure the preservation of the species and although these extraordinary birds are still on the endangered list, there is hope for their survival.

The bison and the whooping crane clearly demonstrate the fragility of our natural environment and just as clearly they are a testimony to the success of Canada's national parks, for without these lands, this nation's wilderness heritage could become extinct in the foreseeable future.

Until recent times, some regions of Canada have been left undisturbed because of their inaccessibility; in these places it is possible to see at first hand how nature has continued to thrive while maintaining its adaptability, changing slowly, during thousands of years, while remaining healthy. One such region is in the southwestern part of the Northwest Territories – a vast tract of land through which runs the Nahanni River. This country became a national park in 1972 but before that time, when I canoed through it, I found that because of its inaccessibility, the land was naturally conserved and its populations of animals and birds, unaccustomed to the presence of humans, went about their affairs in my presence without showing fear or aggression.

From its humble beginnings deep in the Mackenzie Mountains the Nahanni at first threads its way in a southeasterly direction down the middle of a relatively flat valley that is little more than 1 km from the Yukon Territory. Quietly, gathering water from a multitude of glacier-fed creeks, the river passes into an area of swamp and then enters a region of gradual slopes. Here the land is covered by grasses and sedges and wild flowers in season; scattered birches share the riverbanks with runty willows; white spruce grow tall and straight in dense copses over much of the more favored landscape. On stony slopes clusters of black spruce cling precariously; these are scraggly trees, the tallest no more than 15 m high with a girth of about 20 cm.

For the next 12 km the Nahanni travels with modest bustle but as the valley becomes narrower and the descending creeks wider and swifter, the river attains more girth and has a louder voice; its speed increases measurably. By the time it has traveled 40 km from the swamp, the once quiet stream has turned into a turbulent waterway that gouges a passage through the seemingly impassable mountains.

Approximately 200 km from its source, the Nahanni takes a big dive. Wide and swollen and roaring, it plunges 96 m over the lip of Virginia Falls, its descent almost hidden from view by a great, spreading mushroom of spray and mist that drenches all things in the area. For a distance that is almost twice the height of Niagara Falls, the Nahanni cascades to the foot of the gorge, an awesome and boiling thing that causes the ground to shake and the waters to froth like newly-poured milk. From here, at first thunderous and rough as a heaving sea, it rushes onward for another 20 km, collecting more water; then, with another great roar, it smashes into a narrow, twisted canyon aptly named Hell's Gate. Soon afterwards it meets the Flat River, its major tributary, and here, in a wide area where sandbars have been formed by the currents, the Nahanni slows down slightly. It is still boisterous, but because its course is wider and its bends more pronounced, the current loses some momentum.

After passing the Flat, the Nahanni enters a long, exceptionally deep canyon, makes a pronounced U-turn at a place known as The Gate and soon after becomes somewhat wider and a little calmer, continuing in this way through another deep gorge, and then another, until it finally loses momentum at a place known as The Splits, where its course is divided into a network of serpentine channels that continue for some 50 km. Afterwards, the Nahanni joins the stately Liard River, which begins its own life in the Pelly Mountains of south-central Yukon, flows southwards into British Columbia and then turns abruptly north at Nelson Forks as it prepares to enter the Northwest Territories.

The two rivers meet at the Slavey Indian village of Nahanni Butte and from this point their combined waters flow northeast until they join the great Mackenzie River at the community of Fort Simpson, from where the Mackenzie travels northward until it ends at the Beaufort Sea, 241 km above the Arctic Circle.

Over its entire course, the Nahanni travels through rugged and spectacularly beautiful country that is composed of magnificent mountains, alpine valleys, lowlands, a number of other rivers, lakes and virtually uncountable creeks. Glaciers of blue ice contrast markedly with steaming hot springs and profuse tree growth in a nature-blessed region where 31 species of mammals and 120 species of birds live outside of the influence of man.

More than 320 km of the Nahanni River and its surrounding land have been incorporated into the national park, a region that is bounded in the northwest by the Ragged Range of the Selwyn Mountains, includes part of the Mackenzie Mountains, and ends at the southeast boundary of The Splits.

I spent from June to late September exploring the Nahanni, following nine years of almost constant wilderness travel. I had already canoed such impressive rivers as the Peace, the Liard, the Skeena and the Nass, so I felt confident when I left Nahanni Butte and paddled into The Splits. Soon thereafter, I discovered that the Nahanni was an altogether different kind of river. Adjectives come easily to one who is seeking to describe this wild and dangerous waterway, but mere words cannot really do justice to the river, nor to the land through which it runs. The region is a place of legends, of ghosts. Here, at one time, were said to live a giant, fierce people whom neighboring natives called Nahannis, which means "people over there far away" – an early bit of mythology, the origins of which are lost in time; but the name has also been widely used by both native people and early white explorers to denote a variety of Indian races.

Surrounded by legend, yet rooted in grim fact is the story of the two McCleod brothers who, in the early part of this century, entered the Nahanni with a companion, their quest gold. The companion came out but the brothers decided to winter in the region. They were found later, dead, their heads missing. The how and the why of this tragedy remain as much a puzzle today as they did when Mounted Police officers tried to discover the facts. Proclaiming the mystery on every topographic map are two names: Deadmen Valley, given to a lowland area located between First and Second Canyons, and the Headless Range of mountains.

Soon after I passed through The Splits, I found myself having to paddle vigorously against the relentless current; from that point on, my journey was made in slow stages, at times under my own power, as often having to get out of the canoe and cordelle (tow by line) where the flow was too powerful. Portages were frequent and sometimes long, while running through the deep, long canyons where there was no shoreline often caused me to travel a zigzag course in order to counteract the current.

The journey upstream was tiring, often fearful and always exciting, but no amount of trouble or fatigue could have dampened the pleasure and sense of accomplishment that I felt as I conquered each kilometre of river while experiencing the beauty and tranquility of the country. Indeed, I would not have hurried even if I had been able to do so and sometimes I would stay at some especially favored campsite

for a number of days, particularly when I was in the area of hot springs.

Every afternoon, as the sun was dropping towards the mountain peaks, I would land, unpack my gear and make camp. After the tent was pitched and supper was cooking over the fire – always contained inside a ring of rocks – I would devote myself to local explorations, examining flowers and trees and shrubs and often remaining stock-still while watching an animal or a bird.

One memorable evening a female grizzly and her cub strolled past my tent as they went to drink at the riverside. The great shaggy adult stopped about 30 paces beyond the campfire and raised herself on her massive hind legs while the cub, already well grown, sidled behind her. I remained still. The grizzly whoofed softly, her ears pricked forward, her black nostrils flaring as she siphoned my scent and, most certainly, the odors of the stew that I had just finished eating. As she sniffed, staring with her small and myopic eyes, her upper lip was raised, showing her pink gums and the impressive upper dentures, particularly the two great tusks that flanked the flat, chisel-shaped incisor teeth. Her lower lip, meanwhile, remained in its normal position, its black-lined edge hiding all but the tips of her lower canines. She was obviously curious, probably intrigued by the aroma of stew, definitely unaggressive, yet I was impressed by her bulk and power and I could not prevent my heart from beating at about twice its normal rate. For perhaps 20 seconds we stared at one another while the cub peeped from the shelter of his mother's body. Then the she-bear dropped to all fours, grunted softly to her cub and strolled towards the river, the youngster bouncing along at her heels. They drank, making loud sounds; afterwards, while the mother stared at the far bank, remaining immobile as she did so, the cub played in the shallows, pouncing on imaginary prey and often going right under the water. By timing, they left six minutes after their arrival, the mother bear again leading the way into the trees. For about another minute I listened to the sounds of their passage through the brush, then I had the river to myself again, more or less . . .

Frogs chorused continuously from their hiding places by the water; in the rosy sky, nighthawks uttered their strange, nasal calls and dived, their wings making short explosive sounds as the birds pulled up suddenly; in the nearby scrub, small animals scurried and red squirrels chittered from secure perches in the conical spruce trees. And the river gossiped continuously. Yet, amid all this, there was silence – a placid, peaceful absence of disturbing *noise.*

It was like that throughout my time in Nahanni country. Many animals showed themselves openly: moose, great tall beasts of red-brown color, strode along the shoreline or stood on some sandbar, dripping wet, as they rested before re-entering the current. I saw a number of Dall's sheep, one particular ram sporting a magnificent set of curled horns, several groups of woodland caribou, and three wolverines. And an almost endless array of animals, including timber wolves, showed themselves at least briefly during my nearly four months of travel.

Nor had I ever seen so many different species of birds! Bald eagles were present in good numbers (I counted seven nests), and peregrine falcons were not uncommon.

When I left the Nahanni wilderness, traveling quickly now because I was going with the current, and while frost made the leaves crisp and formed ice on pools and areas of quiet water, I felt a deep sense of commitment to the river and the region through which it ran. As the aircraft that was to take me back to the outside took off from the wide waters of the Liard River, I fervently hoped that the Nahanni country would be conserved for all time. And so it has come to pass.

When I came to Canada from Europe in 1954, I was immediately impressed by the vastness of the country and by the many, different kinds of habitat that exist in it. Of particular interest to me was the accessibility of the wilderness and the fact that during my first summer as an immigrant I could leave Toronto after work Friday evening and spend the entire weekend exploring the world of nature without seeing another human being. This, to a people-weary European, was Nirvana. Then, when winter arrived, I left the city and drove almost 2000 km through northern Ontario and took up a homestead.

So began my love affair with the wild places of Canada, a relationship that has never ended. During the last 28 years I have been privileged to visit 22 of our 29 national parks at least once, some of them before they had been set aside as reserves, and it is my ambition to see the other seven before too long.

Some of our parks, especially the northern ones, are relatively hard to get to and because of their isolation and terrain are perhaps not suitable for those who are not experienced in the ways of the outdoors. But most national parks are easily reached and have something for everyone. Places such as Glacier, Jasper, Banff, Yoho and Kootenay, in the west, contain some of the most impressive scenery in the world; others, like Prince Albert and Riding Mountain, in central Canada, and Georgian Bay Islands, Point Pelee, La Mauricie, Fundy and Terra Nova, in the east, offer their own, unique landscapes and wildlife.

I have related some of my personal experiences in this Introduction in order to stress the need for conservation while giving some brief examples of the kind of wild country that still exists in our land. This, however, is not to say that I favor Nahanni or Wood Buffalo above any other park. Small or large, wherever located, every one of the parks that make up our national system has its own particular fascination, ecology and geography, as will be seen in the photographs and written descriptions in this book.

In conclusion, it should be noted that it is unlawful to disturb plants, wildlife of any kind, trees, rocks, and fossils in all of Canada's national parks. Wildflowers are not to be picked. Feeding, touching, or molesting animals is not allowed. Dogs and cats may accompany visitors, but dogs must be kept on the leash. No permit or vaccination certificate is required.

The people at Parks Canada – part of Environment Canada – who administer our system are, I have found, most helpful to those who need assistance and information. Every park has a resident superintendent and a headquarters, the address and telephone number for which will be found at the end of each description. It is always a good idea to contact local park officials before setting out on a trip, or else to get in touch with Parks Canada, Ottawa, Ontario K1A 1G2, telephone (819) 997-2800.

R. D. Lawrence

NATIONAL PARKS OF CANADA

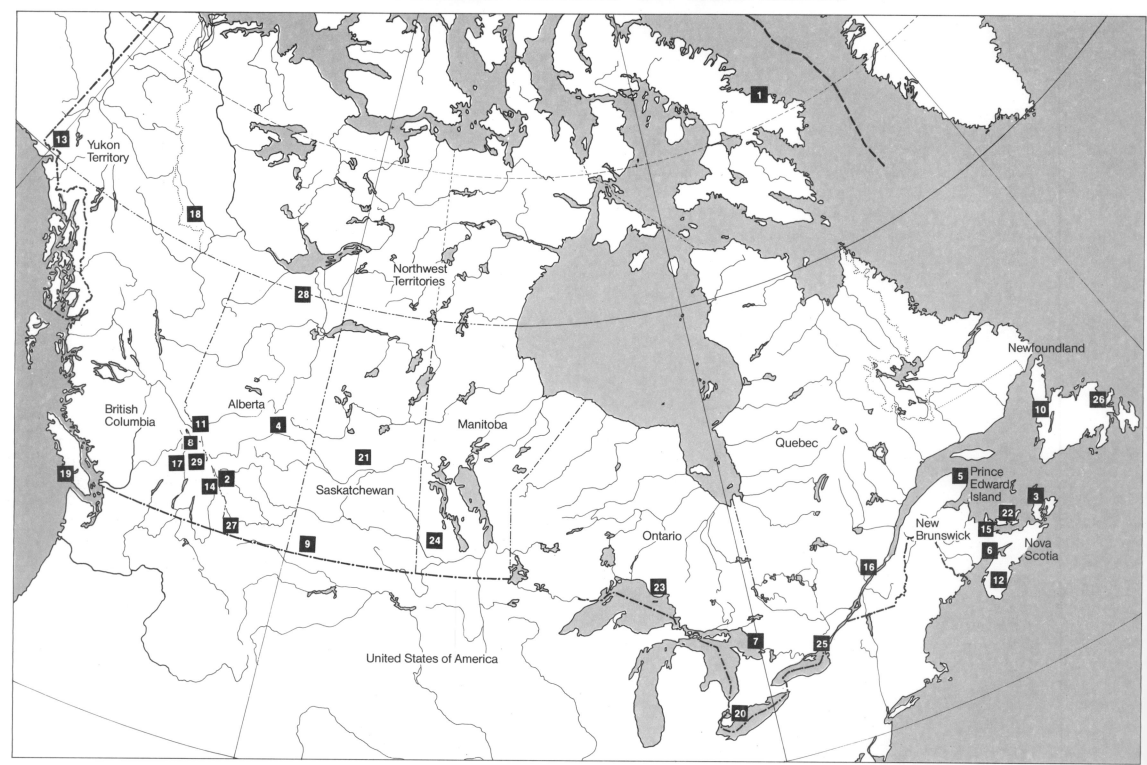

1 Auyuittuq	7 Georgian Bay Islands	13 Kluane	19 Pacific Rim	25 St. Lawrence Islands
2 Banff	8 Glacier	14 Kootenay	20 Point Pelee	26 Terra Nova
3 Cape Breton Highlands	9 Grasslands	15 Kouchibouguac	21 Prince Albert	27 Waterton Lakes
4 Elk Island	10 Gros Morne	16 La Mauricie	22 Prince Edward Island	28 Wood Buffalo
5 Forillon	11 Jasper	17 Mount Revelstoke	23 Pukaskwa	29 Yoho
6 Fundy	12 Kejimkujik	18 Nahanni	24 Riding Mountain	

AUYUITTUQ NATIONAL PARK
Northwest Territories

Canada's northernmost park straddles the Arctic Circle in a region dominated by ice the year round, where winters are long and extremely cold and summers short and definitely cool. This is a land of fierce moods and winds that can gust up to 160 km an hour; but it is spectacularly beautiful.

Located on Baffin Island's Cumberland Peninsula, Auyuittuq (pronounced *ah-yóu-i-tuk*) is dominated by the Penny Ice Cap, an enormous expanse of Precambrian granite mantled by solid ice, the peaks of which rise to 2059 m. This remarkable feature, an unchanging example of the last ice age, covers an area of 5100 km² and has spawned numerous glaciers that flow into the surrounding valleys, one of which – Coronation – is a virtual river of ice 32 km long and 3 km wide. Here, for those visitors hardy enough to challenge the rugged terrain, lies the ultimate natural adventure in a setting that offers scenic grandeur as well as an opportunity to see a wide variety of animals and birds.

Auyuittuq is Canada's third largest national park, encompassing an area of 21470 km², much of which is part of the Penny Highlands and therefore uninhabitable except for deep, U-shaped valleys that form passes in many places. In prehistoric times and during many thousands of years, ice bulldozed over the terrain, carving out the lowlands and creating valleys such as Pangnirtung Pass, which is 97 km long, a canyon that travels a northerly route from Cumberland Sound to Davis Strait at the southern entrance of which the Inuit (Eskimo) village of Pangnirtung is located.

The entire coastline of the Cumberland Peninsula has also been shaped by glaciers that cut into the land below sea level and formed a network of deep and narrow fiords that have walls up to 900 m high. In some places, moraines composed of boulders and stones carried by shifting glaciers dominate the landscape; everywhere and during all seasons ice is commonplace, a feature so striking that in 1975 Parks Canada decided to change the name chosen for this park when it was first established in 1972. The old name, Baffin Island National Park, did not do full justice to the landscape, the climate or the Inuit people who have inhabited the region for thousands of years. After some debate, the present name was chosen – an Inuit word that means *the place which does not melt.*

Auyuittuq is located 2400 km northeast of Montreal, Quebec, and some 664 km due north of the entrance to Ungava Bay, in Labrador. Here is encountered the true north. From May through July, the sun shines 24 hours a day; conversely, in mid-winter, the sun is never seen, a circumstance that causes the land to be shrouded by a darkness that is more blue than black and is further relieved on clear nights by a firmament studded with stars of a brightness never observed in the southlands.

The wind blows almost non-stop, sometimes howling through the passes in hurricane force, at others coming as a relatively gentle, if chilly breeze. At Pangnirtung the average winter temperature is −23°C. and the warmest month, July, has a mean high temperature of 11°C. Because of the climate and the great expanse of permanent ice, there are no trees in the park except for some tiny willows that are only about 30 cm high at full maturing. In season, however, wildflowers are plentiful. Especially during June and July, white mountain avens, yellow arctic poppies and purple saxifrage – to name some – turn the rocky landscape into colorful wild gardens. In the valleys grow Labrador tea, sedges and cotton grass, a plant that fills some areas with white balls that look like newly-fallen snow. Higher locations attract hardy plants such as lichens and mosses and arctic heather.

Because the park is surrounded on three sides by ocean, terrestrial and marine animals are found within its boundaries. In the ocean and along the coast live polar bears, walrus, seals, narwhals, porpoises and whales, including the killer whale; wolves, barren ground caribou, arctic fox, arctic hare, lemmings and weasels are found inland; Canada geese, snow geese, northern fulmars, red-throated loons, eider ducks, peregrine falcons and many other birds also inhabit the region.

AUYUITTUQ: THINGS TO DO

Season: mid-May to mid-September.
Access: Auyuittuq is not easy to get to. Because of its climate and terrain, visitors should be reasonably experienced in wilderness travel.

Regular flights from Montreal touch down at Frobisher Bay, South Baffin Island, from where light aircraft fly to Pangnirtung or to

Broughton Island, another Inuit community north of the park. A 31 km trip from Pangnirtung to the head of Pangnirtung Fiord can be made by Inuit freighter canoe, by snowmobile, or on foot, but boat travel is limited to a short season: ice breaks up about early July at Pangnirtung and early August at Broughton. Inuit guides are available and boats and snowmobiles can be rented. Visitors may also fly in by light aircraft subject to park regulations.

Vehicles: automobiles, hovercraft and other all-terrain vehicles are not allowed in the park and aircraft can land only to drop off parties and equipment at points approved in advance by the park superintendent. Fuel for return flights may be stored at such designated points, but empty fuel drums must be flown out.

Camping: is limited to gravel bars or marked campsites; garbage that cannot be burned must be carried out of the park, for burying refuse is not permitted. There are two primitive campsites in the park: Overlord, at the head of Pangnirtung Fiord (nine spaces) and Summit Lake, 32 km from the head of the fiord (six spaces). There are also six shelters placed in strategic locations of the park; each has a first aid kit; three are equipped with radio-telephones.

Activities: include nature study, hiking, fishing, skiing, photography and climbing. The months of April, May and early June are good for cross-country skiing, snowshoeing and snowmobiling. July and August are the best months for fishing arctic char, which are found in the Baffin Island fiords as well as in interior lakes. Boats can be rented from local Inuit, but visitors must have a territorial fishing licence which can be purchased locally.

It is not permitted to collect any specimens of rock, vegetation or animal life, including bones, fossils or artifacts, but scientific parties may be allowed to study and collect by applying to Parks Canada, Prairie Region, Main Floor, 114 Garry Street, Winnipeg, Manitoba R3C 1G1.

Topographic maps at a scale of 1:250000 are available from: Map Distributing Office, Department of Energy, Mines and Resources, 615 Booth Street, Ottawa, Ontario K1A 0E9; map sheets of the park are: 26I, 26J, 26N, 26O, 26P, 27A, 27B and 16M.

Information on commercial accommodation, transportation and outfitters can be obtained from the Northwest Territories information office: Travel Arctic, Yellowknife, N.W.T. X1A 2L9, Canada.

Park information, including lists of clothing and equipment needed, can be obtained from: The Superintendent, Auyuittuq National Park, Pangnirtung, N.W.T. X0A 0R0, Canada; telephone (819) 437-8962 (satellite call).

BANFF NATIONAL PARK
Alberta

This, our oldest national park, conserves 6641 km^2 of superb wilderness that incorporates more than 400 km of the Rocky Mountains, a landscape characterized by rugged, snow-capped peaks, but at the same time containing great lowland valleys, lush alpine meadows, lakes, rivers and creeks. Variations of terrain encountered here are many and extreme, ranging from glacial mountain tops where no life can exist, to temperate bottomlands that sustain innumerable species of plants and animals.

Banff came into being in 1885 after hot springs were discovered on the northwest slopes of Sulphur Mountain by workers who had been employed in construction of the Canadian Pacific Railway. Following an ownership dispute between individuals who wanted to commercially exploit the thermal outflows, the Canadian government took over the springs and created around them a reserve that consisted of 26 km^2. The present park grew out of that humble beginning. Today, from its southern boundary 130 km west of Calgary, to the northern point where it adjoins Jasper National Park, 370 km west of Edmonton, this magnificent reserve allows visitors to see at first hand the many ways by which nature regulates the ecology and biology of its countless life forms in order to conserve the whole environment.

With diversity the key to natural survival, it soon becomes evident at Banff that all living things have remained undisturbed for the length of time each needed to adapt to the wide differences of topography and climate that distinguish the region. A brief review of the prehistory of this mountain-dominated park will show this.

The Rockies, which extend from northern Alaska to central New Mexico and form the spine of our continent, came into being in the latter part of the Cretaceous period, which began about 135 million years ago during the Mesozoic Era. At the beginning of the period, North America had become largely submerged, flooded by two bodies of water. One of these spread north from the Gulf of Mexico to be met by another that flowed southwards from the Arctic –

circumstances that formed a vast, inland sea that divided our continent in two, lengthwise.

Coniferous trees were already common at that time and the first flowering plants, including forests of oak and maple, had begun to develop. The Rockies, Andes, Alps and Himalayas were formed during the Cretaceous about 75 million years ago while the ancestors of today's birds were flying over a warm but slowly cooling land on which lived recently-evolved, archaic mammals.

It is estimated that the first of the four ice ages that were to change the landscape, biology and climate of North America began about six hundred thousand years ago and that the last occurred some twenty thousand years ago. These glaciations sculptured the Rocky Mountains, caused the extinction of some mammals and plants and gave rise to a number of more specialized life forms. But the last ice age is, in effect, still going on, represented now by the glaciers and icecaps found in the far north and on the peaks of high mountains in more southern latitudes. Many of these can be seen at Banff; they are the remnants of vast sheets of ice, nearly 1 km thick, that once covered the land and carved the fantastic shapes seen on many of the mountains in the park.

The great Columbia Icefield, the largest sheet of prehistoric ice found on our continent south of the Arctic, is a perfect example of the last ice age. Shared now by Banff and Jasper National Park, Columbia extrudes a number of glacial tongues – or flows – that creep down into the lowlands of both parks.

All glaciers produce meltwaters during the frost-free seasons. These carry with them particles of mineral-rich, crushed rock, that impart a beautiful, turquoise color to the park lakes, the best known example being Lake Louise.

The glaciers also impose a wide range of climatic conditions in mountain country; as a result of this, the succession of plants seen in Banff compares to the sequence of vegetable life found on the land as it advances north, where the longer, colder winters have increased the rate of specialization in all species. The many kinds of evergreens in Canada are a good example of this; all of them are hardy trees that continue to grow during winter, though at a reduced rate because they developed the ability to expel the water from their cells at the approach of the cold season, converting the remainder of their contents into a gel that will not freeze, a process known as winter-hardening. Despite this, and while some evergreens are hardier than others, none can survive at extreme altitudes, or in the far north.

In Banff and our other mountain parks, the bottomlands are heavily treed except in locations where grasses and lowland flowering plants have obtained a foothold. In such areas, alpine forest and prairie grassland come together, a phenomenon that causes higher altitude flowers to blossom within sight of plants that are characteristic of plains country. Lodgepole pines, a species that first colonizes the land after fire has swept through it, are common on slopes where the soil is deep and well-drained; so are Douglas firs and limber pines. Other trees found on lower slopes and in valleys include trembling aspen (white poplar), birches and some black poplars, while white spruce march up-mountain until prevented from going higher by the barren ground and extremes of cold, mixing in some areas with Engelmann spruce and larches, the latter being the only conifers that shed their needles in autumn.

Above the tree line, the vegetation is either totally absent or stunted and shaped by the constant winds, but many small, beautiful alpine flowers bloom profusely during the short summer season.

Because the country contains examples of mountain, prairie, lowland forest, and arctic systems, the animal life in Banff is also representative of these four habitats, each species having developed its own requirements, but in some cases sharing the same ranges, especially during seasonal migrations.

Mammals represented in the park include grizzly and black bears, cougar, timber wolf, coyote, fox, lynx and smaller predators; grazing animals such as moose, elk, woodland caribou, mountain goat, bighorn sheep and deer occupy a variety of habitats according to their needs and seasonal influences, sometimes wandering into campsites or standing beside the roads and highways, unconcerned by the presence of humans and automobiles.

Bird life is represented by many species from spring to autumn but during winter only the hardy, permanent residents are found in the forests and valleys. Of these, the most notable are the gray jays, chickadees, nuthatches and woodpeckers, all of which seem to be forever busy as they search for food. Great ravens fly high over the land or perch in the trees, gossiping to each other and sometimes filling the woods with their astonishingly varied repertoires. During the frost-free season, bald eagles are often seen and the golden eagle, a bird that is becoming rare on our continent, also nests within the park's boundaries.

With so many people visiting Banff – and all other national parks – conflicts between humans and animals are likely to occur and although the majority of these are potentially of more harm to individual animals, some may pose serious danger to visitors. For these reasons, and as much for the protection of people as for the protection of wildlife, the following advice should be kept in mind – and it applies to all of Canada's parks and forested regions:

It can be stated with confidence that wild animals in North America do not seek confrontations with humans. Indeed, under normal circumstances, most animals are quick to avoid such contact. But the same cannot be said for man, who is fascinated by wild creatures and will go to considerable lengths to see them – part of the reason why so many individuals visit the parks. Many of us seek sightings of mammals and birds as eagerly as others collect rare stamps or coins; and provided that we are satisfied with watching from a respectable distance, such an occupation is harmless, stimulating and of great educational value.

Problems arise when we try to get too close, or when we attempt to handle small creatures, or the young of large species. By doing so, we stand a chance of being attacked by the animal, by its parent, or, more usually, of frightening the animal to such an extent that it can panic, rushing away to find shelter and perhaps injuring itself or, if young, straying out of its home range and dying as a result.

All large wild mammals are *potentially* dangerous. Those armed with fangs and claws, such as the bears, are quite able to kill a human, but even grazers like moose, elk and deer can inflict serious injury if molested, or during the mating season. Moose cows, for instance, are protective of their calves and have been known to attack intruders, and bulls in the rut have charged and treed hunters; elk bulls share this mating aggression and have even been seen to charge automobiles and trucks.

Small animals like ground squirrels and chipmunks can, if handled, inflict deep wounds with their razor-blade-sharp incisor teeth and even quite young predators can do a lot of damage with tooth or claw, to say nothing of the injuries that their infuriated mothers can cause if they happen to be nearby – and they usually are.

Many animals in Banff and other parks have become accustomed to people and will allow themselves to be approached more closely than they countenance in the deep wilderness; however, wild they remain and they will not tolerate intrusion beyond the limits they have set. This poses a problem, of course, since only a bear or a moose knows what those limits are! The wise visitor will therefore admire or photograph from a distance, allowing the animal the personal space that it needs and is usually prepared to defend.

Park animals that have become accustomed to humans should not be fed by visitors. Apart from the fact that feeding bears or other mammals is unlawful, it can be dangerous – especially when the sandwich or cake is finished. The food may be gone but its odor still clings to the visitor and is easily detected by the animal, which may then attack without warning.

Bears, because they are so well armed and so powerful, are especially to be avoided. Like all other animals, each bear has individual characteristics and traits that cannot be readily detected by inexperienced observers. This makes them unpredictable.

Both the grizzly bear and the black bear are found in Banff. The grizzly is more dangerous but the black bear, because it adapts easily to human presence and is nearly as powerful as its bigger relative, can also do great damage. Attacks by both species have taken place in which people have been killed.

Most attacks by grizzlies occur when a human unwittingly surprises the bear. For this reason, it is always a good idea in grizzly country to carry a noisemaker of some sort: a tin can containing small stones, or a bell. Sound will alert a grizzly to human presence and it will most likely leave the trail without being seen. These bears, because they fear no other creature – and have no need to – are likely to take a nap almost anywhere. If an unwary visitor should round a bend in the trail and virtually stumble on a dozing grizzly, the animal will probably attack. This *has* happened.

Most black bear attacks, on the other hand, have resulted from feeding the animals, or from a person approaching a cub too closely, or walking between the cub and the mother.

Attacks on visitors to our parks are by no means common. Indeed, considering the numbers of people that go through the parks system each year, confrontations of this kind are rare. Advice in the form of pamphlets is available at the park entrances; if it is heeded, people and animals will remain at peace.

BANFF: THINGS TO DO

Season: Banff is open all year but some visitor services are seasonal.

Camping: facilities are provided at 11 campgrounds, the largest being Lake Louise, Tunnel Mountain, Two Jack Lake and Johnston's Canyon. Daily fees vary and depend on whether sites are serviced or not. Camping space is allocated on a first-come-first-served basis. Campgrounds open about mid-May, close September 15, depending on weather. Maximum allowable stay in a campground is two weeks. It is not permitted to camp outside established campgrounds, but people on overnight trail trips may bivouac en route, provided they register. Campsite permits must be purchased for all types of campgrounds except primitive ones. Picnic areas and wayside tables are located along highways. A variety of commercial accommodation is also available. Details obtainable at all information centers.

Motorboats: may be used on the Bow River, near Banff townsite, and on Lake Minnewanka, but should conform with federal regulations and carry proper safety equipment.

Snow vehicles: must stay on trails designated for their use; all other motorized land vehicles are restricted to public roads.

Hiking: more than 1100 km of trails provide access to all areas of the park. Many lead to remote sections and are suitable for overnight trips; other trails are suitable for day hikes, or riding, particularly those in the Lake Louise or Moraine Lake areas. Maps and a guide to the trails can be obtained at information centers.

Mountain climbing: is popular at Banff, but climbers and overnight hikers must register with a park warden before and after each trip.

Fishing: is allowed in the park, but a permit must be obtained from the information centers or the administration office.

Facilities: most facilities offered by any modern town are available at Banff townsite, situated beside the Trans-Canada Highway. Visitors will also find a variety of recreational facilities, including swimming pools, bus and boat tours, riding stables, sightseeing gondola lifts, a golf course and ski developments.

Fires: are allowed only in the fireplaces provided for this purpose, or in portable stoves. Barbecues may be used only in campgrounds or picnic areas and all coals must be dumped in existing park fireplaces. Fire permits must be obtained from a park warden or interpretation center for any open fires during trail travel. Unattended fires should be extinguished if found by anyone in any part of the park. If fire is out of control, it should be immediately reported. These regulations also apply to *all* parks.

More information on Banff National Park can be obtained from: The Superintendent, Banff National Park, Box 900, Banff, Alberta T0L 0C0; telephone (403) 762-3324.

(See also Jasper, Kootenay and Yoho national parks and the Introduction).

CAPE BRETON HIGHLANDS
Nova Scotia

Geological upheavals and climatic erosion combined to produce the great plateau that is the main land feature of this park, a table that rises 360 m above the sea and is mostly covered by large bogs, dry barrens, ponds and small lakes. Occupying about 90 per cent of Cape Breton Highlands National Park, the moor has been further shaped by a network of rivers and creeks that over the centuries have carved a number of irregular gorges and deep valleys, some of which are made distinctive by modest but scenic cascades.

Created in 1936, this was the first national park in the Atlantic provinces, a reserve located on the northern part of Cape Breton Island that contains 950 km² of land and is bounded on the west by the Gulf of St. Lawrence and on the east by the Atlantic Ocean.

Apart from the fact that the park protects some of the last remaining wilderness in Nova Scotia, it is also historically notable, for it lies just south of Aspy Bay, where John Cabot first landed on the shores of North America in 1497. Marking this event is the Cabot Trail, which rises from the edge of the sea to climb up Mackenzie Mountain, from where it continues along the flat top of this landmark. Visitors may drive or hike this popular route which in 1981 brought almost one million visitors to Cape Breton Highlands. Along the coasts, bold headlands, hidden coves, beaches and steep cliffs meet the ocean's surf, forming a land-sea habitat shared by marine and terrestrial life.

The plateau itself supports a wide variety of vegetation, from plants and flowers normally found in the far north, to heath plants on the bogs and stunted balsam firs and black spruce on drier crests. In the more temperate valleys grow sugar maples, yellow birch and beech;

white spruce is the predominant species found on the coastal slopes.

Animal life in the lowlands is typical of that found in eastern Canada, including moose, white-tail deer, black bear, bobcat and fox; on the highlands live small numbers of pine marten, lynx (and possibly a few isolated cougar, or mountain lion). Bird life is extensive. To date 230 species have been counted. In the lakes and rivers are found eastern brook trout; Atlantic salmon annually spawn in these waters while marine fishes and mammals are found on both coasts.

CAPE BRETON HIGHLANDS: THINGS TO DO

Season: sections of the park are open year round.

Hiking: some 200 km of hiking trails run through spectacular scenery – both the interior plateau and along the edge of the sea; 300 m viewpoints overlook the valleys and coasts.

Camping: the park offers a total of 850 campsites in a number of campgrounds, some of which have heated service buildings with showers, individual three-way hook-ups and landscaped sites. Others are more primitive, containing pit privies, fire grills and a source of water. Private campgrounds are located at Ingonish and Cheticamp.

Swimming: there are two supervised beaches in the park and a number of unsupervised salt and freshwater beaches. Facilities include changehouses, toilets, picnic tables and playgrounds in some locations.

Fishing: purchase of a National Parks fishing licence allows visitors to angle for trout and salmon in the streams and lakes.

Golf and tennis: the Highlands Links offers a challenging 18-hole game. Tennis players can use three paved courts located in the Ingonish Beach day-use area.

Interpretive program: includes a variety of roadside signs, exhibits and self-guiding, interpretive trails. In summer, day events such as guided walks and evening talks are offered. Programs for organized groups can be arranged in advance.

Winter activities: include cross-country skiing, snowshoeing and snowmobiling in the forests and valleys.

Facilities: communities near the park provide a full range of services, including doctors, hospitals, dentists, restaurants, garages, stores and churches.

For more information on Cape Breton Highlands National Park contact: The Superintendent, Cape Breton Highlands National Park, Ingonish Beach, Cape Breton, Nova Scotia B0C 1L0; telephone (902) 285-2270.

ELK ISLAND
Alberta

Located about 35 km east of downtown Edmonton, this park is an island only in a symbolic sense, for it is what might be termed an oasis of nature surrounded by a landscape completely altered by man. About one quarter of its total of 195 km^2 lies south of Highway 16, the Yellowhead Route that runs from the boundary of Saskatchewan all the way to Prince Rupert, British Columbia, on the Pacific Coast; the other three-quarters of the park, including Tawayik and Astotin lakes – the two largest found on the reserve – extends almost due north for 22 km, ending just south of Highway 15. Only four other national parks are smaller, but Elk Island is fascinating as a conservation milestone.

The first known inhabitants of the area then called Beaver Hills were the Sarcee Indians, a people who lived off the land and in harmony with it; but with the advent of the fur trade, the Cree, firearms poised and seeking new trapping and hunting lands, displaced the Sarcee. There followed an era of biological destruction spurred by Europeans who clamored for more and more furs. The balance of nature was altered by the trap and the gun.

By the late 1800s, the beaver, like the bison, were almost exterminated. The country was nearly empty of life and full of black scars left by fires that got out of control after settlers burned their land in order to clear it. Gone were the large stands of spruce, larch and poplar so essential to the once plentiful elk that were by then also close to extinction.

Shortly after the turn of the century, local conservationists petitioned the federal government to set aside an elk preserve in the Beaver Hills. In 1906, Elk Park was established with an area of 41km^2. This became a dominion park in 1913 and a national park in 1930, growing progressively throughout the years and continuing to play a key role in the conservation of dwindling wildlife species.

Elk Park was eventually renamed Elk Island National Park, a sanctuary that today contains representative examples of the natural life that once thrived in the Beaver Hills region; but outside its boundaries lies a vast expanse of land dominated by agriculture and industry, bisected by highways and liberally sprinkled with towns.

At first, in addition to the protection it offered to the plants and to a variety of animals natural to the region, the park was famous because it contained the only herd of purebred, plains bison *(Bison bison)* in Canada (see Introduction). The Canadian government had imported bison from the United States and settled them in Elk Island, later releasing most of them in Wood Buffalo Park. There, the plains animals mingled with remnants of the only herd of woods bison *(Bison bison athabascae)*, left in Canada. This resulted in the crossbreeding of both species so that for years, conservationists believed that the purebred woods bison had become extinct.

But in 1957 biologists of the Canadian Wildlife Service discovered a small, isolated herd of them in a remote area of Wood Buffalo National Park. These woods bison had been prevented from mingling with the plains bison by impassable terrain and Wildlife Service staff transferred some of them to Elk Island, where they were resettled south of Highway 16 and isolated from their plains relatives by fencing. Since that time, this herd has been used to seed small groups of woods bison in suitable wilderness ranges. Some of the animals recently relocated in the area of Nahanni Butte, Northwest Territories, appear to have settled there, others of the same herd have migrated to neighboring ranges of their own choosing.

In addition to elk and the two kinds of bison, moose, deer, lynx, coyote and beaver are among the 35 species of mammals that are now found on the reserve. The land itself has been colonized by fire-influenced poplars in pure stands and by forests in which evergreen and deciduous trees are intermingled. In other areas are meadows and wetlands that contain wildflowers in season as well as examples of a variety of other plants and shrubs. Bird life is also well represented. In winter, the hardy species found over most of Canada are present in good numbers, but from spring to autumn more than 200 species of birds use the park.

ELK ISLAND: THINGS TO DO

Season: although the park is open all year, most services are of a seasonal nature.

Camping: is limited to two areas: Sandy Beach, a semi-service site available on a first-come-first-served basis, and Oster, a more primitive site for organized groups who have made reservations. Maximum stay at either campsite is two weeks. During autumn, winter and spring, Sandy Beach is closed, but a small primitive campsite is open at Beaver Bay. Oster campground may be used by skiers and snowshoers during the winter.

Commercial accommodation is available at Edmonton, Fort Saskatchewan, 25 km west, and at Lamont, 5 km north of the park.

Interpretive program: visitors may track elk, or listen to campfire legends that impart a better understanding of the park. These and many other activities are presented by interpreters. A program schedule and posters advertise events well in advance. For details, contact park staff at the information center, at the south gate, or at the administration building located on the west shore of Astotin Lake.

Hiking and walking: a variety of trails, or abandoned wardens' tracks give visitors a chance to stroll off the roads and into the park's wilder areas. There are also two self-guiding trails that are less strenuous, and a trail along the south shore of Astotin Lake. To avoid losing their way, hikers should check with wardens or interpreters for accurate route information before using old warden trails.

Picnic facilities: are located at Sandy Beach, Beaver Bay and Tawayik Lake. Group picnic facilities are also located at Sandy Beach.

Swimming facilities: are at Sandy Beach and include a changehouse and shower and a supervised swimming area. *Note:* it is natural for lakes such as Astotin to have algae and leeches, which make swimming in such waters unpleasant at certain times of the year.

Fishing: prohibited in the park because its lakes and ponds support only minnows and sticklebacks.

Boating: canoes and sailboats only are allowed on Astotin Lake. Motorboats are prohibited in the park.

Fires: are permitted in designated fireplaces only. Visitors seeing untended campfires are asked to co-operate by extinguishing them. Fires that are out of control should be immediately reported to park staff.

Skiing and snowshoeing: are ideal ways of enjoying Elk Island and its winter wildlife. Several well-marked ski trails are maintained in the park.

Other facilities: include a buffalo paddock that may be toured by car and a nine-hole golf course located opposite the entrance to the recreation area.

West of the Recreation Area there is a beaver pond exhibit where visitors can sit and watch beaver at work. Several occupied lodges are visible from the viewpoint and a short trail leads across a beaver dam and along a beaver-inhabited pond.

More information can be obtained from: The Superintendent, Elk Island National Park, Site 4, R.R. 1, Fort Saskatchewan, Alberta T8L 2N7; telephone (403) 998-3781.

(See also the Introduction.)

FORILLON
Quebec

It is difficult at first to see any connection between Forillon National Park, in the Province of Quebec, and the State of Alabama, in the southern United States. But if the geological history of North America is consulted, it shows that the park and the American state respectively contain the northernmost and southernmost terminals of the Appalachian Mountain range.

Formed during the end of the Permian period more than 200 million years ago, the Appalachians end (or start, as the case may be) with the Gaspésian Mountains in Forillon, itself located on the very tip of the Gaspé Peninsula. This narrow, pointed strip of land juts into the Gulf of St. Lawrence and the park occupies most of it – a spit of 35 km long by 17 km wide at its base that encompasses 240 km² of land; its continuous marine boundaries make approximately 80 km.

Located 724 km east of Quebec City, this reserve is accessible via Highway 132. Its northern coastline faces the Gulf of St. Lawrence, its southern shores face the Bay of Gaspé, while its easternmost point, a finger-like projection 5 km long by less than 2 km wide at its broadest part, ends at Cape Gaspé.

Because of their intimate contact with the Atlantic Ocean, the climate, life forms and shores of this park continue to show its influence. For many thousands of years, the sea has combined with climatic forces to shape the peninsula: at ocean's edge, the land is in places rugged, containing rough-sculpted crags and promontories; in other locations are found long, pebbled beaches, craggy cliffs that stand 200 m above the sea, sandy beaches and small coves protected by rocky capes.

Three major plant communities found at Forillon are of particular interest; two of these are maritime: the flora of the saltwater marsh found at Penouille, a wedge-shaped cape that forms a relatively large and sheltered bay and, within this same shelter, the plant life of the neighboring sand dunes. The third community is inland and offers examples of arctic-alpine vegetation that are survivors of the last ice age. Besides these scientifically important species, the park contains a large number of other plants that grow in a variety of habitats, such as evergreen and deciduous forests, mixed forests, and meadows. Fresh water is available in five small lakes and a number of rivers and streams, all of which maintain different kinds of plant communities.

Wildlife is plentiful and varied at Forillon. Each summer, thousands of sea birds nest in the park, particularly on the cliffs that rise on the northern shore of the headland. Here congregate large numbers of gulls, double-crested cormorants and guillemots, while more than 200 other species of birds also use the park during frost-free seasons.

Mammals are represented by 32 distinct species, some terrestrial, others maritime. Inland live moose, deer, bear, lynx, fox and other eastern animals. From May to October, many kinds of whales rise in the surrounding waters and it is often possible to see and hear these great animals when they blow, exhaling plumes of misty breath before gulping down fresh supplies of oxygen. Gray and harbor seals are attracted to the coast by the abundance of fish and by the presence of flat rocks on which they rest and take the sun, while the sea itself contains an endless number of typically marine animals like molluscs, crustaceans, urchins and stars, to name but a few species.

The first European known to have sailed into the Bay of Gaspé was Jacques Cartier, who took possession of the land in 1534 in the name of France. Before that, Micmac and Iroquois natives summered in the area now occupied by the park, attracted there by the abundance of fish and marine mammals. After Cartier, French, Portuguese and Spanish fishermen dared the might of the Atlantic in order to get the codfish that was abundant in Gaspésian waters.

Today, interpretive programs offered by the park staff narrate the history of the region and stress the fact that man lived in Forillon in close harmony with the sea and the land up to the turn of the century.

FORILLON: THINGS TO DO

Season: sections of the park are open all year.

Hiking: an extensive network of trails allows visitors to explore all the interesting aspects of this fascinating land.

Photography and painting: artists with brush or camera will find much to occupy them in a place where land and sea create inspiring landscapes while at the same time offering subjects for the wildlife enthusiast.

Swimming: many sandy beaches are ideal for swimming. A sandy point in the Bay of Gaspé is protected from the wind and is a safe, well-equipped beach ideal for family enjoyment.

Skin diving: the coast offers many ideal skin diving locations. A diving suit is compulsory. Services for divers are available in the city of Gaspé, 35 km from the park. Registration at two toll booths is compulsory for every dive.

Scenic cruises: private boats take visitors along the northern coast of the peninsula to watch seal colonies and other marine life. A guide accompanies the cruises, which leave from Le Havre.

Fishing: sea and freshwater fishing is within the reach of all. A National Parks licence is required for trout in the streams and lakes of the park. Sea fishing is available from all wharves and by private boats available at Le Havre.

Winter activities: Forillon is open during winter months for snowshoeing and skiing along good trails. It is also possible to do some winter camping after authorization by the park superintendent.

Camping: about 325 semi-serviced campsites, on three sites are available. No reservations. There are also wilderness campgrounds, a group campground, and equipment for the handicapped in the Petit-Gaspé sector. Private camping and hotels are available in the surrounding villages.

More information can be obtained from: The Superintendent, Forillon National Park, Box 1220, Gaspé, Quebec G0C 1R0; telephone (418) 368-5505.

FUNDY
New Brunswick

Rising gradually from a line of rugged, wave-pounded cliffs, the land occupied by Fundy National Park climbs to a rolling plateau that is a remnant of a prehistoric range of mountains known geologically as the Caledonia Highlands. Averaging about 300 m above sea level, this undulating tableland is cut in a number of places by deep valleys of steep, rocky walls where waterfalls are common and beautiful and where the predominant colors come in pastel shades of greens and mauves and blues spiced by the browns of stone and soil.

Covering an area of 206 km², this park on the south coast of New Brunswick skirts the Bay of Fundy for 13 km and extends inland for slightly more than 14 km. The reserve and the region in which it lies is associated with some of Canada's earliest history. In 1604, Samuel de Champlain visited the bay and claimed it as part of the French colony of Acadia, which was later to become Nova Scotia. In 1784, the present province of New Brunswick separated from Nova Scotia and in 1825 the first colonists settled in what was to become the village of Alma, the community adjacent to the park.

Located 143 km west of Saint John, the park is accessible by road via Highways 1, 2, and 14; and from Moncton by Highway 14. The only public transportation to the reserve is a bus from Moncton that covers the route daily except for Sundays and holidays.

The landscape of Fundy is bold and dramatic. Above the ocean it offers sylvan glades and lush forests, but at the foot of its cliffs the ageless sea continues to pound and scrape and shape the rocks during stormy times, or to lap gently at the shingle and ancient granite when the weather is calm. Here are found tides that are among the highest in the world, a phenomenon accounted for by the pressure of water coming in from the Atlantic Ocean that is trapped by Chignecto Bay on the one side and by Nova Scotia's Minas Basin on the other. As a result, tidal differences vary from 6 to 12 m, a twice daily, spectacular series of changes that dominate the lowland and marine environments.

Visitors can stroll along great tidal flats at low water in areas such as Alma, Point Wolfe, or Herring Cove and see a variety of marine organisms that await the incoming tide in such shelters as small pools, under rocks, and among seaweeds. Later, a grand view of the high tide is offered at Herring Cove.

Animals found in the park include moose, white-tail deer, an eastern race of coyotes, beaver, porcupines and a number of other, smaller species. A few black bears travel through the park, but are not reported to be resident in it; but there have been periodic sightings of the eastern cougar, an animal that until recent years was thought to be extinct in this region.

More than 200 species of birds have been recorded on this reserve; some 90 species nest in the park and can best be observed in the early mornings from May to the middle of July, when breeding males sing melodiously. Bird checklists are available at information centers located on the reserve. In addition to the nesters, because the Bay of Fundy's shoreline is a migrating route, large numbers of species stop over in the park.

This reserve, created in 1948, is open all year, although services are seasonal, most visitors arriving between May and September. Snowshoeing and cross-country skiing are two of the activities that can be enjoyed in winter.

FUNDY: THINGS TO DO

Season: sections of the park are open year round.
Boating: motorboats are permitted on the Bay of Fundy, but are prohibited on all park lakes and streams. Rowboats are permitted; they can be rented at Bennet Lake. Canoeing is feasible on several of the small lakes.
Arts and crafts: the province of New Brunswick operates an arts and crafts school in the park each summer for adults and children: for more information write to the Department of Culture and Youth, Fredericton, New Brunswick.
Hiking: is the best way to explore the park. More than 80 km of trails are maintained.
Fishing: is permitted in all lakes and rivers. A National Parks licence is required.
Facilities: during summer season, swimming in a heated, saltwater pool is popular; in addition there is a nine-hole golf course, tennis courts and a lawn-bowling green. There is a restaurant-coffee shop, souvenir shop, a motel and chalets.
Camping: facilities are provided at three campgrounds: Chignecto, Point Wolfe, and at park headquarters; fees dependent on whether site is unserviced or equipped with electrical, water, and sewer connections. All sites allocated on a first-come-first-served basis and are open the third week of May and close the first week of October·

limited facilities are available during winter.

More information on Fundy National Park can be obtained from The Superintendent, Fundy National Park, Alma, New Brunswick E0A 1B0; telephone (506) 887-2000.

GEORGIAN BAY ISLANDS
Ontario

Seven Canadian painters who banded together and eventually became known as The Group of Seven have made famous the scenic grandeur of Lake Huron's great bay on which the islands of this park, and 30000 more, are located. Great rock formations, massive white pines shaped by wind action and deep, clear water that reflects the blue of sky or the gray of cloud are major characteristics of this region.

The park is small, containing only 13.8 km^2 that are divided among 50 islands, or parts of islands, scattered along 62 km of the Georgian Bay coastline from Macey Bay to Moose Deer Point.

Beausoleil Island, the largest of the reserve group, is about 8 km long by 1.6 km wide; it lies just off Honey Harbour and is visible from the town of Midland. This island is the interpretive hub and the focal point of Georgian Bay Islands National Park. It is also one of the last refuges of the Massasauga rattlesnake, an endangered species that, though poisonous, is protected. This snake is mild-tempered and prefers a quiet life in swampy areas where its food is located. It should not be disturbed or killed.

Flowerpot Island, the next largest, lies 144 km to the northwest, off the tip of the Bruce Peninsula. Its outstanding features are formations that resemble the flowerpots from which it takes its name. They have been formed by strong wave action and receding water levels. The largest of these is 15 m high, the smallest 9 m. The island itself is steeped in Indian legend and was once the place of ancient taboos.

The natural environment of this park is complex, exhibiting as a main feature on its southern islands hard granite and gneiss rock that has changed little during the last 8000 years. Vegetation is varied, in some places spotty because of the barren rocks, in others consisting of bushes, ferns and wildflowers, in yet others dominated by the big pines.

GEORGIAN BAY ISLANDS: THINGS TO DO

Season: most of the park is open year round.

Access: to all camping, day-use, picnic and swimming areas can be attained only by boat, so for those visitors who trailer their own craft, launching ramps and parking facilities are available at commercially-operated marinas in such centers as Midland, Penetanguishene, Honey Harbour or, for Flowerpot Island, at Tobermory. Water taxi services and boat rentals are also available.

Interpretive program: this provides an insight into how climate, water, islands, plants and animals are interrelated; guided walks, group discussions, films and slide shows as well as displays at the interpretive center near Cedar Spring add to the interest and knowledge of visitors.

Camping: is confined to only a few islands, the main sites being on Beausoleil, where 11 areas furnish 186 spaces. The largest ground is at Cedar Spring, located near the main dock north of Papoose Bay; this provides 87 sites with piped water, natural spring, showers, flush toilets, kitchen shelters, stoves, fireplaces and picnic tables. The other camping spaces on the island provide tent pads, dry pit toilets, stone stoves, picnic tables and in some cases kitchen shelters. Primitive campsites are found at Thumb Point, Tonch Point, Sandpiper Bay, Little Dog, Minnehaha, Bone Island and Islands 92 and 95B. Stay is limited to a maximum of two weeks; there is no reservation. Docking and mooring facilities for cruisers and sailboats are available at Cedar Spring, Ojibwa Bay, Lost Bay, Bone Island and Fryingpan Bay. Maximum tie-up time at any one dock is 48 hours.

There is a group campground at Cedar Spring in operation from May 15 to September 15, dates variable according to weather conditions.

Primitive camps are open year round, accessibility depends on ice conditions on Georgian Bay. From December through March, winter camping, snowshoeing and cross-country skiing are popular.

The eastern sector of the park is accessible from Midland and Penetanguishene along Highway 12, or from Honey Harbour at the end of Highway 69 and Muskoka Road Five. Flowerpot Island can be reached from Tobermory at the end of Highway 6. The general area is within about two hours' driving from Toronto.

More information can be obtained from The Superintendent, Georgian Bay Islands National Park, Box 28, Honey Harbour, Ontario P0E 1E0; telephone (705) 756-2415.

GLACIER
British Columbia

The landscape of Glacier National Park is as rugged as any found in the west. This region is heavily influenced by the Selkirk Mountain Range, a system of high peaks, icefields, heavy precipitation the year round, and spectacular vistas. Along a narrow strip on the eastern side of this reserve, west of the town of Golden, the rounder and smoother slopes of the Purcell Mountains make the land less demanding, give rise to larger and more lush valleys and encourage a wider range of wildlife than is found in the rest of the park.

Containing 1350 km² of wild country, the park was first created in 1886, five years after the discovery of Rogers Pass, which is located on the northeast corner of Glacier and is today bisected by the Trans-Canada Highway, which travels from its junction with Highway 93, in Banff, to Golden and Revelstoke and thence to Vancouver. Originally, the park contained only 76 km², but by 1911 it had been expanded to its present proportions.

Glacier is an ideal place for the experienced, outdoor enthusiast and mountain climber but visitors need not be skilled alpinists nor rugged nature buffs in order to explore and enjoy the beauty of this region; they can, instead, hike over a variety of less demanding trails, or stop at a number of viewpoints along the way.

The park's eastern boundary comes down a jagged ridge between two streams running through a fairly wide valley that is partly treed and partly barren, spotted by sandy eskers and marked by landslides. From here a view to the northeast shows the tops of some very high mountains located in Hamber Provincial Park; to the southwest rise the jagged peaks of the north end of the Hermit Range, always partially snow-covered. Mount Shaughnessy is the highest; its white summit looms above the treed slopes that parallel the Beaver River Valley.

A few kilometres west of this park entrance there is a viewpoint where visitors can see Sorcerer Mountain, which raises its snow-and-ice-covered head 3166 m above sea level in the extreme, northwest corner of the park, about 35 km distant. Farther west, at another viewpoint located on the outside of a long curve in the highway, an extended series of rock-cuts are worthy of note. These show gray-green *schist,* a type of rock that probably began as fine mud on the bottom of a sea that existed in this region more than one billion years ago. The mud solidified to form rock and was probably subjected at some point in time to great pressures which reorganized and reconstituted its minerals, forming tiny crystals of mica.

From the same observation point, the wooded Beaver River Valley is seen to travel in both directions, offering views of bare-topped Prairie Hills and, to the south, Bald Mountain, both of which are part of the Purcell Range. These peaks show the contrast that exists between the sharply defined, avalanche-scarred Selkirks and the far more rounded tops of the Purcells.

The highway travels about 40 km through Glacier and contains other viewpoints and stops of interest, thus offering visitors excellent photographic opportunities and allowing them to experience the awe-inspiring scenery of the park from the comfort of their cars.

Animal and vegetable life in many areas of the park are naturally influenced by the extremes of topography and climate. Avalanches are frequent; spring, summer and autumnal rains often lash the peaks and valleys. In winter, the snowfalls are heavy and deep, in some years accumulating to a total depth of 23 m.

Bears, because they seek suitable shelters and sleep through the cold season, are plentiful in the park. Indeed, Glacier is famous for its populations of grizzly and black bears, which should remind hikers to proceed with caution while in the habitat of these animals. Large grazers such as moose and deer are present in the reserve but are not common. Woodland caribou are also found within its boundaries, as are smaller mammals; but because more than half the park is located above the 1900 m level, where the land is stark and treeless and where many glaciers cause the temperature to fall even in summer, this reserve is less likely to yield frequent sightings of animals and birds.

GLACIER: THINGS TO DO

Season: sections of the park are open all year.
Hiking: 140 km of established trails wind through the park and hiking them is the best way to appreciate the beauty of the region. Many of the trails switchback steeply up and down mountainsides, leading to glaciers or snowfields. All climbers, glacier travelers and overnight hikers must register with park wardens at the administration office – located in the community of Glacier on the Trans-Canada Highway and in the approximate center of the park – before and after every trip. Topographic maps and a hiker's guide are available at the administration office.
Fishing: is permitted, but few fish are found in the silt-laden waters. A National Parks licence is required.
Camping: three campgrounds are open through the summer: Loop Brook, Illecillewaet, and Mountain Creek. The first site is located 5 km west of Rogers Pass Summit; it has 20 spaces, kitchen shelter, flush toilet, firewood; trailer limit: 3.7 m; the second camp is 2 km from Rogers Pass Summit and has 58 sites, two kitchen shelters, flush toilets, firewood; trailer limit: 3.7 m; Mountain Creek is 21 km west of Rogers Pass Summit; it is the largest, with 306 sites, including 46 trailer spaces, four kitchen shelters, flush toilets and trailer sewage disposal.
Picnic sites: are adjacent to the Trans-Canada Highway and are open from May to October. Some offer educational displays.
Naturalist program: features self-guiding trails, roadside signs, informative publications and conducted hikes held during the summer. A schedule of events is available at park outlets.
Winter camping: Illecillewaet campground is open for winter use for those who wish to hike and ski in the park. No fee is charged during this season, but campers must register at the Glacier administration office.
Ski-touring and snowshoeing: is some of the finest in Canada, although frequent avalanches make many areas hazardous. Anyone traveling off the highway in winter must register at the Glacier administration office. Trails are neither packed nor groomed.
Snowmobiles: the park is closed to these vehicles.
Fires: may be lit only in fireplaces provided. To light fires in back-country, hikers must obtain a permit from the park wardens at Glacier administration office. Barbecues may be used at designated camp-grounds and picnic areas only and coals must be dumped into park fireplaces.
Other facilities: accommodation, groceries and gas are available in the park at Rogers Pass, east of the park at Golden, and west of the park at Revelstoke.

More information can be obtained from: The Superintendent, Glacier National Park, Box 350, Revelstoke, British Columbia V0E 2S0; telephone (604) 837-5155.

(See also Mount Revelstoke National Park.)

GRASSLANDS
Saskatchewan

Canada's 29th national park is not yet open to the public and although its debut is not expected before the second half of the 1980s, its historic, geographic and biological uniqueness deserve a place in this book.

In June, 1981, the governments of Saskatchewan and Canada signed an agreement that calls for the establishment of a reserve that will eventually encompass 907 km^2 of prairie land located on the Canada-United States border between the towns of Val Marie and Killdeer, in southwestern Saskatchewan. The first of these lands to be placed in the public domain will consist of two blocks, each of which will contain 95 km^2.

This region is about 125 km south of the Trans-Canada Highway; the Val Marie block will be accessible from Swift Current via Highway Four South; the Killdeer block from Moose Jaw, via Highway Two. From the U.S., Route 242 from Malta, Montana, leads north to Val Marie; Route 247 from Glasgow, in the same state, travels north to Killdeer.

Historic Frenchman River, known locally as Frenchman Creek, is one of the main features of the Val Marie, or western, block; the eastern block will include badlands of unique topography that were shaped by erosion of sedimentary rock, among them "The Sinking Hill," a sandstone upheaval that has formed over the last 35 years. This is approximately 11 m high (in 1982), but the ground around it is sinking at the rate of 30.5 cm a year.

Hot summers, cold winters, dry winds and low precipitation are typical of this semi-desert area where the landforms, vegetation and animal life have been heavily influenced by the climate. Rare species of plants and animals live here; dogtown and squirrel-tail grasses are examples, as is the short-horned lizard. Other unusual wildlife species include the only black-tailed prairie dog colonies found in Canada, prairie falcons, greater prairie chickens, ferruginous hawks, golden eagle, sage grouse and Richardson's hawk. This, too, is the home of the pronghorn antelope.

Fossil bones of the three-horned dinosaur, Triceratops, and those of ancient crocodiles have been found near Frenchman's River, a waterway that, historically, was once the camping place of Sitting Bull and the Sioux who sought refuge in Canada after they defeated Colonel George Armstrong Custer's famed Seventh Cavalry.

These are but a few of the fascinating things that will attract many visitors to the new park when it opens to the public.

More information can be obtained from: Parks Canada, Ottawa, Ontario K1A 1G2; telephone (819) 997-2800.

GROS MORNE
Newfoundland

This park on the west coast of the Island of Newfoundland contains land forms that are counted as some of Canada's most geologically interesting and visually spectacular. Incorporating 1942 km^2 of the Great Northern Peninsula, which parallels the Gulf of St. Lawrence, Gros Morne's Long Range Mountains run from Cape Ray, in the southwest corner of the island, to the northernmost tip of the province, ending at the Strait of Belle Isle and facing Labrador. The park is located midway along this range, its southern boundary incorporating Bonne Bay, its northern limit ending just past Shallow Bay.

The Long Range Mountains were formed in prehistoric times and were exposed to the grinding forces of ice during four glaciation periods as well as to countless thousands of years of climatic erosion. These forces combined to reshape the entire range, reducing the heights and carving features such as the fiord-like ponds of Western Brook, Baker's Brook, and St. Paul's Inlet as well as the Tableland on the south side of Bonne Bay. In later ages land gradually rose from the sea – and is still rising – to form the coastal plain that lies between ocean and mountain.

Apart from its rugged geological past, this part of Canada is also rich in human history. Three pre-European cultures lived within its boundaries as early as 2500 B.C. The first is now recognized as the Maritime Archaic Indian age that began in 2500 B.C. and is thought to have ended about 1500 years later. Artifacts excavated indicate that these people lived mainly on marine mammals and caribou. There is also evidence that Dorset Eskimos flourished here between 1 and 700 A.D. The third culture was represented by the Beothuk, who inhabited Gros Morne from about 800 A.D. until the last of these people died in St. John's in 1829, a small clan that became victim of white as well as Indian aggression.

Animals found in the park include moose – not native to the province of Newfoundland – caribou, black bears, lynx, beaver and, in the most barren parts, the arctic hare. Birds are more plentiful and varied; common and arctic terns, herring gulls and large, black-backed gulls are characteristic of the coast; willow and rock ptarmigan are typical birds of the heathlands and barrens.

The plant life of this reserve is complex and diverse, influenced as it is by the ocean, many types of bedrock and soil, and its range of elevations. The land between high and low tides contains extensive growth of brown seaweeds as well as Irish moss, a kind of red seaweed. On coastal areas exposed to the sea are found wind-shaped, stunted balsam firs and white spruce. The extensive wetlands of the coastal plain are mostly covered in sphagnum bogs and here grows the insect-capturing pitcher plant. The lower slopes, which have been extensively logged, are now covered in many places by dense groves of second-growth balsam fir and white birch, while the exposed moraine ridges and the higher slopes support shrubby heath vegetation, stunted black spruce and mountain alder.

GROS MORNE: THINGS TO DO
Season: sections of the park are open all year.
Interpretive program: provides a variety of events, information about which can be obtained at the visitor reception center near Rocky Harbour. Included in this program are movies and a video center, visits to Lobster Cove Head Lighthouse for exhibits of seashore life, conducted hikes, short walks, campfire talks, evening shows and demonstrations.
Hiking: during summer the well-developed trail system and the Long Range Mountain Plateau are popular among seasoned and novice hikers alike. The trails have primitive camping facilities.
Camping: several campgrounds are located in the park, the largest being Berry Hill, which has 156 sites with washrooms, kitchen shelters, showers and trailer dumping stations. Picnic areas throughout the park allow visitors to enjoy the scenery of the Long Range Mountains, the Tableland, the coastal plain and the rugged coastline.
Fishing: Atlantic salmon and trout provide excellent fishing in the freshwater areas of the park. Many also enjoy cod fishing in the ocean. Provincial regulations apply.
Swimming: several areas are suitable for swimming for those who like water that is permanently on the cool side of 14°C.
Winter activities: abundant snowfalls in the park area provide excellent skiing, snowshoeing and snowmobiling. Winter camping areas have been designated for overnight use.
Facilities: motel, guest homes, private campgrounds and a full range of services – including medical and hospital – are available in communities immediately adjacent to the park.

Gros Morne National Park is located 126 km north of Corner Brook and is accessible via Highways 1 and 430.

More information may be obtained from: The Superintendent, Gros Morne National Park, Box 130, Rocky Harbour, Bonne Bay, Newfoundland A0K 4N0; telephone (709) 458-2417.

JASPER
Alberta

Jasper, created in 1907, is one of four contiguous reserves in the west that form what has become known as The Four Mountain Park block. Jasper, Banff, Kootenay and Yoho occupy a protected area of 20160 km² that straddle the Continental Divide. Yoho and Kootenay lie along the western side of the Rocky Mountains; Jasper and Banff are on the eastern side.

A complete cross-section of the Canadian Rockies is represented by the four reserves, each of which contains excellent examples of the types of geology, climate, vegetation and wildlife associated with the Western, Main and Front ranges, the major systems of the Rockies in this region that are largely formed of sedimentary rocks such as limestone, shale and sandstone, all influenced by glacial scouring and climatic erosion.

Visitors who tour all four parks can readily see the differences that exist in these ranges. The Western system consists of rock that is greatly fractured and folded; the Main shows uplifted and slightly tilted rock; the Front, formed later than the others, shows rocks that are severely folded and that contain many faults.

Jasper is the largest of the four parks, containing 10878 km² of which only 800 are valleys. These scarce flatlands are most suitable for visitor use, but they are also essential to the survival of many of the animals of the reserve and for this reason some areas have been set aside as wildlife sanctuaries. The northward-flowing Athabasca River is the major drainage system through the park. It rises in the mountains immediately southwest of the reserve and flows for 1231 km to empty into Lake Athabasca on the southeastern boundary of Wood Buffalo Park.

In a region well watered by rivers and creeks that are constantly fed during the frost-free season by the melt from glaciers, the vegetation below tree line is particularly lush. Lodgepole pines, poplar, white spruce and Douglas fir are the most common species on the lower slopes. Engelmann spruce and alpine fir are found on higher elevations. Above the timberline, at about 22100 m, the sub-arctic climate has stunted the vegetation, though hardy species of shrubs and flowers brighten the otherwise grim landscape during the short growing season.

Black bears are a common sight along the roadways, open woodlands and in or near campgrounds; the grizzly prefers the more isolated upper areas, sharing this habitat with mountain goat, bighorn sheep, Marmots and pikas, small relatives of the rabbit that live year round in the high country. Moose, elk and mule deer browse on the lower slopes and meadows and it is not uncommon for a couple of prime bull elk to decide to take a rest in sight of a busy campground.

Birds found in Jasper include eagles, pipits and ptarmigan at higher altitudes, while gray jays, ravens, magpies, chickadees and nuthatches are the most often seen at lower elevations. A check-list of species found in the reserve is available at the information centers.

The Columbia Icefield, located in the southwest corner of Jasper and spilling over into the northwestern boundary of Banff, is a striking feature of both parks and a dominant climatic factor in the region. So are the hot springs found on both reserves, which serve to remind visitors that although the high points of our world are perpetually cold, the center of our planet is fire-hot, containing an incandescent mass of molten rock called magma that in places becomes vented into the crust of the earth, creating volcanic activity or hot springs.

Jasper National Park is easily reached from all points of the compass. The Yellowhead Route (Highway 16), leads into the heart of the reserve from the northwest and from the east; Highway 5 in British Columbia connects with the Yellowhead at Tete Jaune Crossing, while the Trans-Canada Highway from Calgary and from Golden in British Columbia (No. 1), links with Highway 93, which travels north through Banff and ends at Jasper Townsite.

JASPER: THINGS TO DO

Season: all year, with facilities curtailed in winter.

Hiking: 1000 km of trails in this reserve make it a hiker's paradise in summer and in winter offer excellent cross-country skiing and snowshoeing. Topographic maps, trail guides and current condition of routes may be obtained at the information centers.

Camping: although limited to designated locations, there are 1826 spaces available at ten campgrounds, the largest, with 758 sites, is Whistlers. Sites are allocated on a first-come-first-served basis; maximum stay is two weeks at one site. Full-service season runs from about mid-May to about mid-October, depending on weather.

Fishing: a $4 National Parks licence required. Fishing is best in waters not clouded by silt.

Boating: rowboats or canoes are allowed on most of the ponds and lakes; motorboats are allowed only on Pyramid and Medicine Lakes.

Snow vehicles: may be used only on designated trails; permits required and snowmobilers must also register at the warden office, where information about trails is available.

Other activities: include hot-springs bathing, downhill skiing, swimming, golfing, tennis, horseback riding, boat and bus tours, and a tramway.

More information can be obtained from: The Superintendent, Jasper National Park, Box 10, Jasper, Alberta T0E 10E; telephone (403) 852-4401.

(See also Banff, Yoho and Kootenay national parks.)

KEJIMKUJIK
Nova Scotia

Waterways are the main feature of this park, which was named after its largest lake when it was created in 1968. Somewhat rounded in shape, the 381 km² contained by Kejimkujik (pronounced *ke-jim-kóo-jik*) are peppered with more than two dozen lakes, the majority connected to one another by streams and creeks.

Mixed woods cover three quarters of the forested land. On dry locations grow red maple, red oak, white birch and some white pine; red spruce and balsam fir are found in wetter areas, while coniferous forest covers about one fifth of the remaining landscape.

Ancient rocks, flattened by erosion, are the reserve's underlay, in some areas consisting of slate and quartzite, in others granite. The land itself was bulldozed and smoothed by glaciers, which also raised many low, oval hills and scoured shallow basins in the bedrock; these, when warmer climates melted the ice sheets, filled with water.

Black bear, bobcat, otter, mink, beaver and white-tail deer make their home in the park. Birds are also well represented by such species as flycatchers, vireos, boreal chickadees, spruce grouse and warblers; common loons, common mergansers and great black-backed gulls are present on the larger lakes; those interested in fishing will find in the waterways yellow and white perch and brook trout.

Kejimkujik is located 150 km southwest of Halifax and is accessible via Highways 103 and 8. Few roads are found in the park, but trails are plentiful and canoe travel is easy and the best way to see this reserve.

KEJIMKUJIK: THINGS TO DO

Season: sections of the park are open all year.
Canoeing: is probably the most popular form of recreation. Jake's Landing has boat launching facilities and canoe rentals; the quiet waters of the Mersey River are suitable even for inexperienced paddlers.
Swimming: Kejimkujik Lake, with its intriguing shoreline, is at one and the same time the center for exploration and swimming. Here are found changehouses, picnic sites, lifeguards, and playgrounds.
Interpretive program: visitors are encouraged to stop at the Reception Center at the park entrance to obtain help to plan their visit and to learn about the various interpretive facilities and programs offered.
Camping: Jeremy's Bay Campground has 329 sites that are semi-serviced, but there are many small, primitive campgrounds located in various parts of the reserve, which is open year round. Jeremy's is in operation from mid-May to mid-October; winter campsites are located near Jake's Landing. A campsite for organized youth groups is located at Jim Charles Point; special rates available; pre-registration required.

More information can be obtained from: The Superintendent, Kejimkujik National Park, Box 36, Maitland Bridge, Annapolis County, Nova Scotia B0T 1N0; telephone (902) 242-2770.

KLUANE
Yukon Territory

Two thirds of Kluane's (pronounced *klu-áh-nee*) 22015 km² are dominated by Canada's highest mountains and much of its awesome wilderness lies under sheets of prehistoric ice, but this unique park is nevertheless a place of thriving life and spectacular scenery. All of the land occupied by the reserve lies above the 60th parallel, its southern and western limits bordering on Alaska and in some areas only 15 to 50 km from the Pacific Ocean, a geographical position that influences lowland climate and causes high precipitation. Winters are long and severe, with heavy snowfalls; summers are short but can be hot, with a fast growing season. The roar of fracturing ice and the constant gurgle of rushing waters fill the spring with sound, while the advent of autumn, with frost increasing nightly, signals the beginning of the quiet time in this region of splendor and isolation.

Getting to Kluane is half the adventure and is not cheap, but every kilometre traveled and every dollar of cost are amply repaid by the experience. Some visitors fly to Whitehorse, the capital of the Yukon Territory 158 km east of the reserve, then travel to the park in rented automobiles. Most people drive the Alaska Highway, traversing this fascinating road from either north or south; others take a ferry from points south, sailing in comfort through the Pacific's Inside Passage (a most rewarding journey) and then motoring in their own vehicles from Haines, Alaska, to the main park entrance at Haines Junction, Yukon, a distance of 256 km.

The wilderness of this reserve is dominated by two mountain

systems that run W-N-W by E-S-E: the Kluane Range, closest to the Alaska Highway, throws up an unbroken, serried chain of peaks that average more than 2000 m in height; the St. Elias Mountains, farther to the southwest, tower above their neighbors, climbing up to 6050 m at Mount Logan, in the southwest corner of the park; this is Canada's highest peak.

The summits of the St. Elias Mountains and those of the adjoining Icefield range – part of the same system – accommodate the largest icefield found anywhere outside of the polar regions, while between these peaks and the Kluane Range runs a lowland trough called the Duke Depression that is composed of a succession of valleys and plateaus and watered by many glacier-fed rivers and lakes.

Three types of vegetation distinguish this region. Vast evergreen forests are common in the lowlands and up to 1200 m above them; next in gradient succession grow birches and willows and shrubs, either singly, or in small clusters on land that is carpeted by a mat of small plants that produce colorful, sub-alpine flowers. Above this, at altitudes that vary between 1500 and 2000 m, the tundra is encountered. This term, borrowed from Russian, characterizes land that is permanently frozen a few feet below the surface as a consequence of which frost is likely to occur at ground level at any time during the summer. Plants and animals of the tundra have acquired special traits in order to adapt themselves to their inhospitable environment; as a result, while populations of individuals may be exceptionally numerous, kinds, or species, are greatly reduced. Summers here are characterized by uncountable mosquitoes, caribou, birds and a gorgeous carpet of small flowers that blend vibrantly with green mosses and paler lichens.

Kluane is inhabited by a wide variety of mammals and birds and although many of these are also common to other parts of the American continent, some of the species found on this range are exceptional. Here live Canada's largest moose, majestic animals darker than their southern counterparts and some of which may weigh more than 800 kilos; sharing the same habitat are record-size timber wolves. Grizzly and black bears, wolverine, lynx, coyotes, Dall's sheep, mountain goat, beaver and a variety of other carnivorous and herbivorous mammals also inhabit lowland and mountain up to the most barren heights. Birds are well represented in the park. To date, 170 species have been recorded, including the peregrine falcon, eagles, willow and rock ptarmigan, thrushes, magpies and a variety of warblers.

KLUANE: THINGS TO DO

Season: sections of the park are open year round.

Camping: is limited to Kathleen Lake, where there are 41 sites and a day-use area. But there are a number of territorial campgrounds located on both the Haines and Alaska highways that border the park. Commercial accommodation is available at Haines Junction and Destruction Bay.

Mountain climbing: only experienced climbers should attempt the high peaks. The most challenging and famous are: Logan, Steele, Lucania and Kennedy.

Fishing: good angling exists for rainbow and lake trout, Arctic grayling and land-locked salmon.

Hiking: 250 km of trails offer excellent hiking for the experienced and beginner alike. Binoculars and cameras will add to the trips. Guided hikes are offered by park staff, including one to a rock glacier and another to an old glacial lakebed.

Winter: camping, cross-country skiing and ice fishing are all feasible.

Because the Kluane wilderness is exceptionally rugged and its climate unpredictable, those interested in visiting this park should seek advice beforehand, especially if they intend to go on overnight trips or on special expeditions. Lists of clothing, food and emergency equipment are available from park authorities.

The best time to see the reserve is between June 15 and September 15, when temperatures range from a high of 28°C to a low of 5°C.

All hikers planning to stay overnight in the backcountry must register with a warden or at either of the two information centers before entering the wilderness. They must also check back with the park on completion of the trip.

More information is available from: The Superintendent, Kluane National Park Reserve, Haines Junction, Yukon Territory Y0B 1L0; telephone (403) 634-2251.

KOOTENAY
British Columbia

Located on the western slopes of the Rocky Mountains, this park is bisected by two wide river valleys, the Vermilion and the Kootenay. Here are found the headwaters of the Kootenay River, a waterway that ultimately flows westward to empty in the Columbia River and thence into the Pacific Ocean off the coast of Oregon.

Alpine lakes, deep canyons, high glaciers, hot springs and distinct vegetation zones are major features of this reserve's 1378 km² in which visitors can gain some understanding of four natural themes: mountain building, landscape sculpturing and the history of the remarkable examples of flora and fauna found within the park.

Created in 1920, Kootenay National Park is accessible via Highways 1 and 95, the former leading to the reserve from either east or west, the latter running north from Missoula, Montana, and ending at Highway 1 in Banff National Park, which lies adjacent to Kootenay, but on the other side of the Rockies. British Columbia communities near the reserve include Cranbrook, Kimberley and Invermere to the south, and Revelstoke and Golden to the northwest. The distance to Vancouver is 800 km.

The major plant communities found here are alpine-tundra, sub-alpine Engelmann spruce, sub-alpine fir, and interior Douglas fir and the animals native to the region include Rocky Mountain bighorn sheep, mountain goats, moose, white-tail deer, mule deer, elk, cougar, timber wolves, grizzly and black bears as well as a wide variety of bird species.

Kootenay is a highway-oriented park where canyons spaced out along the major travel route furnish magnificent views of the two main valleys, both of them rimmed by high mountains. Visitors can also see pictographs here, along with wildlife and plants, and enjoy hot spring bathing.

Just inside the northern entrance to the park are found the "paint pots," ochre beds that at one time were the source of the vermilion paint used by the Kootenay Indians to decorate themselves as well as their belongings. In addition to this, some of the special viewpoints allow visitors to observe and photograph avalanche slides, animal salt-licks, waterfalls and goats climbing the slopes of Mount Wardle.

Kootenay has a less severe climate than its neighboring mountain parks, especially in its southern region where summers are hot and winters mild, owing to the proximity of the Columbia River Valley. But because Kootenay lies adjacent to Yoho National Park, where large glaciers influence the climate, its northern area is subject to somewhat longer, colder winter conditions.

KOOTENAY: THINGS TO DO

Season: sections of the park are open all year.
Camping: 512 campsites are contained by five campgrounds: Marble Canyon (61); Redstreak (241); Crook's Meadow (100); McLeod Meadows (100); and Dolly Varden Picnic area (10).
Hiking: many trails offer excellent opportunities for sightseeing, photography, picnicking and wildlife observation.
Hot springs: visitors may relax at the famous Radium Hot Springs Aquacourt, open all year.
Fishing: good trout fishing is available in the park.
Boating: unpowered boats and canoes may be used on the Kootenay River with permission of the park superintendent.
Winter activities: cross-country skiing and ski-touring trails are available and snowshoeing is a popular activity.
Commercial accommodation: is available at Radium Hot Springs and Vermilion Crossing.

More information can be obtained from: The Superintendent, Kootenay National Park, Box 220, Radium Hot Springs, British Columbia V0A 1M0; telephone (604) 347-9615.
(See also Banff, Jasper and Yoho national parks.)

KOUCHIBOUGUAC
New Brunswick

Kouchibouguac (pronounced *koo-chi-boo-ak*) was the term used by the Micmac Indians of New Brunswick to describe the river that runs through this park. It meant *the river of long tides,* an apt description of the twice-daily fluctuations of the Atlantic Ocean that creep up the coastal waterways, linger for a time, then recede, leaving in their wake a multitude of small, marine organisms and exposed salt flats that are greened by tough grasses and purpled by the flowers of sea lavender.

Running offshore for 25 km is a necklace of sandbank islands that for centuries have protected the fine, sandy beaches that lie along the coast of Northumberland Strait, an arm of the Gulf of St. Lawrence that curves around the shores of Nova Scotia and New Brunswick and is shielded on the north side by Prince Edward Island. The beaches, marshes and lagoons found on the eastern face of the park are backed on the landward side by forests interspersed with bogs, cedar swamps and meadows, while the gently rolling Kouchibouguac, St. Louis and Black rivers keep the vegetation well-watered and give rise to a wide variety of shrubs, mosses and flowers, including pitcher plants and 25 species of orchids.

This reserve, established in 1969 and encompassing 226 km², is an intricate blend of sea, coastal flats and inland habitats inhabited by a wide variety of animals and birds. Common terns form a colony that is considered one of the largest in North America; osprey, the park symbol, nest in the reserve, as do piping plovers; during the migratory seasons, tens of thousands of shore birds stop to rest here before continuing their long flights to north or south.

Gray and harbor seals are a common sight off the mouth of the St. Louis River; the lagoons and salt marshes nurture and protect countless species of small, marine organisms, while the forests shelter moose, deer, black bear, beaver, fox, hares, groundhogs and many other mammals common to eastern Canada. The waters of the park team with such fish as striped bass, eel, flounder and brook trout and extensive clam beds in tidal sands' allow visitors to enjoy this succulent ocean product just for the digging.

KOUCHIBOUGUAC: THINGS TO DO

Season: sections of the park are open all year.
Camping: from May to October the South Kouchibouguac campground accommodates both tents and recreational vehicles; 143 sites are issued on a first-come-first-served basis. Washroom, showers, a kitchen shelter, playground, dumping station, individual fireplaces and firewood are available. Organized groups can reserve in the Group Tenting area, but only tents and bedrolls are allowed.
Interpretive program: summer daily activities include exhibits at Kelly's Beach, evening programs and campfire circle, mobile puppet theater, special children's events, canoe paddling, bicycle trips, and bird-watching excursions.

Hiking: many shoreline, beach and woodland areas offer excellent hiking trails.
Swimming: many swimming areas are found in the park. Kelly's Beach has a canteen, changehouses, showers, washrooms and picnic area as well as interpretive signs and exhibits.
Canoeing and boating: the rivers and lagoons of the reserve offer ideal waters for canoeing, boating and kayaking.
Winter activities: a summer bicycling trail is turned into a groomed cross-country ski trail in winter, offering trail-side shelters with wood stoves and picnic tables. Snowshoeing, tobogganing and an annual ski marathon are popular events.

Kouchibouguac National Park is located 100 km north of Moncton, New Brunswick, and can be reached via Highways 11 and 117. Communities adjacent to the reserve offer a full range of services, including serviced campsites during summer and winter.

More information can be obtained from: The Superintendent, Kouchibouguac National Park, Kouchibouguac, Kent County, New Brunswick E0A 2A0; telephone (506) 876-2443.

LA MAURICIE
Quebec

This park of 544 km² was created in 1970 and well represents the Laurentian Highlands: an undulating landscape of rounded hills, lush forests in pure and mixed stands, a network of rivers and innumerable lakes. Picturesque waterfalls are common along the courses of some waterways and because the reserve lies in the boundary zone between northern evergreen trees and the more southerly St. Lawrence lowlands where deciduous trees are common, 25 species of hardwoods and 10 species of conifers are found here. La Mauricie is an ideal place in which to canoe and camp while fishing for speckled and lake trout, bass, or pike. But it is also a place of sylvan trails, clean, sparkling beaches, profuse wildflowers and abundant mammals and birds.

Accessible via Highways 55 and 351 and located 200 km north of Montreal, the entrance to the park marks the end of surrounding fields of the inhabited rural region and leads the visitor along a good, scenic road that winds through the reserve. This route is remarkable for its ever-changing and always captivating scenery and for the fact that it crosses the three main valleys that run through the forests.

Lake Wapizagonke, probably the most picturesque, runs for 10 km on the western side of the park, ending 5 km south of Lake Antikagamac. Both bodies of water resulted from the same geological forces that formed the Laurentian Mountains, as succeeding upheavals followed by glaciers and radical climatic changes combined over millions of years to carve the hills and lowlands.

LA MAURICIE: THINGS TO DO

Season: sections of the park are open year round.

Camping: during the summer, three campgrounds offer a total of 539 sites. In the southwest is the Mistagance campground; some distance north is the one on Lake Wapizagonke; in the southeastern section is the Rivière à la Pêche campground. All include washrooms and water outlets, fireplaces at each site and a central supply of firewood.

Fishing: season extends from the last Sunday in May to the end of August. Daily catch limit set at five fish.

Canoe-camping: a number of routes containing primitive camp-grounds allow canoeists to explore the backcountry. Permits are needed. Fires are allowed only in fireplaces at campsites along Wapizagonke Lake; elsewhere, canoeists must use portable stoves.

Hiking: many trails penetrate the forests, wander through the hills and down to lakes and rivers. Picnic sites are available at a number of locations.

Swimming: excellent beaches are found at almost all lakes.

Interpretive program: many activities have been organized for visitors. Naturalists are available at interpretation centers.

Winter: there are 70 km of marked and groomed cross-country trails. Snowshoeing is popular and camping is available.

Other facilities: full services are available in towns and villages surrounding the park.

More information can be obtained from: The Superintendent, La Mauricie National Park, Box 758, Shawinigan, Quebec G9N 6V9; telephone (819) 536-2638.

MOUNT REVELSTOKE
British Columbia

This reserve, located 17.7 km west of Glacier National Park and also within the Selkirk Mountains, is smaller than its neighbor but no less interesting. Established in 1914, Mount Revelstoke's 263 km^2 consist of a blend of valleys covered by rain-forest vegetation where giant cedar and hemlock trees grow profusely, of sub-alpine slopes on which stand tall, straight Engelmann spruce and firs, of large meadows above the 1800-m line that are carpeted with bright flowers in season and, at the peaks, of tundra country – an area of permafrost carpeted during the short summer by small shrubs and plants.

Accessible from west and east via the Trans-Canada Highway, this park offers visitors a unique experience: they can drive to the top of a mountain by following the Summit Road, a gravel drive that starts near the city of Revelstoke, making twists and switchbacks for 26 km to a point high above this splendid wilderness region. Along the way, scenic lookouts furnish unsurpassed views of the landscape, including the Columbia and Illecillewaet river valleys and the Monashee Mountains.

Four natural areas distinguish this reserve. The bottomlands contain examples of the Columbia Forest, where the great cedars and hemlocks tower over a thick understory of devil's club, alder and ferns and where black bears and ravens are common; sub-alpine forests begin at the 1300-m elevation; here, the tall spruce and firs shelter populations of red squirrels, blue grouse and gray jays; above 1800 m are the meadows where the forest thins out and the climate becomes more severe. In this habitat live Columbian ground squirrels and hoary marmots. From the meadows to the peaks lies the tundra, forbidding areas of rock and ice and permafrost where hardy plants like saxifrage and grasses find sparse existence and where caribou and mountain goat share the range with pikas and golden eagles.

MOUNT REVELSTOKE: THINGS TO DO

Season: sections of the park are open all year.

Camping: no campgrounds are provided in the park but private grounds are located along the Trans-Canada Highway east and west of the reserve. There are many picnic areas and scenic lookouts.

Hiking: more than 65 km of hiking trails wind through the park. Topographic maps and trail guides are available at the park administration office. All mountain climbers and overnight hikers must register in and out.

Fishing: cutthroat and brook trout are found in Eva and Miller Lakes; rainbow trout are caught in Upper and Lower Jade Lakes. A permit is required.

Interpretive program: conducted walks and hikes led by park naturalists are held daily during summer in neighboring Glacier National Park.

Skiing: several areas are suitable for cross-country skiing; two loop trails are groomed and packed; one is 2 km long, the other 5 km. Snowmobiles are allowed only at the Summit Road; permits required.

More information may be obtained from: The Superintendent, Mount Revelstoke National Park, Box 350, Revelstoke, British Columbia V0E 2S0; telephone (604) 837-5155.

(See also Glacier National Park.)

NAHANNI
Northwest Territories

In 1978, this park became the first natural site selected for the UNESCO (United Nations Educational, Scientific and Cultural Organization) World Heritage List in recognition of the outstanding universal value of the reserve; this tribute to the magnificent wilderness contained by Nahanni's 4765 km² came not much more than a decade after the great river that is the major characteristic of the region had been coveted as a site for hydro-electric power.

It is to the everlasting credit of the Canadian government that this unspoiled, remarkable example of our country's natural heritage was conserved in 1972; and although Nahanni National Park is accessible only by water – or by air from Watson Lake, Yukon Territory, or from Fort Simpson, in the Northwest Territories – and therefore visited by relatively few people its creation has added greatly to this nation's park system.

Nahanni is not for the faint-hearted. And it is expensive to reach. But those who see this rugged and beautiful example of Canada's unspoiled north are forever enriched by the experience. Whether traveling up the South Nahanni River, or down it, no one can remain unmoved in the presence of a land that contains so many remarkable features as well as so many examples of fauna and flora.

Virginia Falls, the awesome cataract that plunges 96 m over a precipice of rocks to deluge the surrounding area with moisture, is twice the height of Niagara. The power of its rushing waters makes the ground quake and the noise of its descent can be heard several kilometres up- or downstream. Three steep, smooth canyons, one of which rises almost 1000 m and is 20 km long, are monumental examples of geologic sculpturing, while the turmoil and roar of the river as it smashes into a figure-eight canyon known as Hell's Gate have the ability to intimidate and exhilarate at one and the same time.

Moose, Dall's sheep, grizzly and black bears, wolves and a variety of other mammals wander unmolested through the wilderness, sharing the land with eagles and hawks and ravens and many more species of birds. Bottomlands are covered in places by dense forests of white spruce, or in almost equally dense stands of balsam poplar; cotton grass raises stalks crowned by white balls that cause some slopes to look as though they have been suddenly covered by a very localized snowstorm. Profuse wildflowers are encountered in valleys and at high altitudes; a number of sulphur hot springs have formed pools where the water is heated to 68°C. and where surrounding vegetation is luxurious. Wild Mint Mineral Springs, in the vicinity of the Flat River – the major tributary of the South Nahanni – have formed crystalline pools of water trapped by tufa (calcium carbonate deposits); Rabbitkettle Hot Springs, in the northwest part of the reserve, have formed fantastic terraces of tufa; one of these, of circular formation, is 61 m in diameter and rises 28 m above the Rabbitkettle River, its center filled with clear, warm water. The terraces surrounding the spring are colored in grays and gold and because they are formed by layers of extremely brittle calcium carbonate, they are exceptionally fragile.

Nahanni National Park has had little traditional development and though inaccessible by road, there are guided raft and canoe tours down the South Nahanni River and jet-boat tours upriver to Virginia Falls. There are no campgrounds in the reserve, but there are seven primitive camping areas equipped with tables, fire grills and pit toilets. The rivers in the park offer superb canoeing for experienced paddlers, but those not versed in white-water canoeing will be wise to portage around the more turbulent stretches of water. All visitors, whether traveling on their own, or guided by outfitters, will have ample opportunity to observe and photograph the spectacular vistas and wildlife of the reserve. Fishermen will find Dolly Varden trout and arctic grayling in tributary streams.

Careful planning is essential for those wishing to visit this park. The region is definitely dangerous and caution must always be observed. Canoes tip easily in the fast stretches of the Nahanni; water levels can rise up to 30 cm an hour; mountain climbing exposes individuals to sudden rock slides and treacherous footing. But knowledge of the area and good planning will ensure accident-free travel and will give rise to experiences that will always be remembered.

Large scale topographic maps are essential. The following cover the park: 95L for Glacier Lake; 95E for Flat River; 95F for Virginia Falls; 95G for Sibbeston Lake. All are available from: Map Distributing Office, Department of Energy, Mines and Resources, 615 Booth Street, Ottawa, Ontario K1A 0E9.

Canadian Pacific Airlines fly regularly to Fort Simpson, N.W.T; Pacific Western Airlines have scheduled flights to Watson Lake, Yukon Territory; from either of these locations visitors can charter light aircraft that will take them to the park. Information on names, locations, fees and services of river outfitters in the area can be obtained from: The Director, Travelarctic, Yellowknife, Northwest Territories.

More information on the park can be obtained from: The Superintendent, Nahanni National Park Reserve, Postal Bag 300, Fort Simpson, Northwest Territories X0E 0N0; telephone (403) 695-3151. *(See also the Introduction.)*

PACIFIC RIM
British Columbia

This reserve on the Pacific Ocean consists of three separate regions of land and sea located on the west side of Vancouver Island. Collectively, these contain examples of ocean beach, coastal islands and rain forest, the first represented by the Long Beach section, the second by the Ocean Group Islands, and the third by the West Coast Trail.

The park was established in 1970 and encompasses a total of 388 km^2; the largest land area is found at Long Beach; the smallest areas are represented by mere rocks that stick up above the water as part of the Broken Group Islands.

The reserve contains some interesting examples of mammals and birds, including marine animals such as northern sea lions, harbor seals, killer, gray, sperm, humpbacked and blue whales, harbor and Dall's porpoises. Land animals are less unusual; black bears, cougars and black-tailed deer are the only large mammals found in the reserve; smaller animals are represented by raccoons, otters, mink, red squirrels, deer-mice and bats.

Birds in the park include such forest species as woodpeckers, Steller's jays, brown creepers, red crossbills and chickadees; shoreline species are represented by red-throated loons, great blue herons, bald eagles, black oystercatchers, varieties of diving ducks, grebes, cormorants, common loons, gulls and murres.

Pacific Rim is a place of heavy rains and prolonged cloudiness; temperature changes occur frequently and rapidly at all times of the year. But the region has a long growing season; this, coupled with plentiful moisture, has given rise to forests of enormous trees. Sitka spruce are found nearest the ocean; cedar, hemlock and fir are the more usual evergreens found inland. Bog and muskeg areas support shorepine, Labrador tea and bog laurel and under the umbrellas of the big trees are thick carpets of salal, salmonberry and huckleberries.

PACIFIC RIM: THINGS TO DO

Because conditions vary widely in the park's three sections, separate lists are given here for each; season is year round.

Long Beach Section
Camping: one semi-serviced campground is located above Green Point; a primitive campsite is located at the northern end of Long Beach.
Interpretive program: consists of conducted walks, self-guiding trails, audio-visual presentations and evening events; from mid-June to September.
Fishing: from boats and from surf allowed. Launching ramps located at Grice Bay, Tofino and Ucluelet.
Hiking: many trails exist along beaches, headlands and woodlands.

Scuba diving: park waters are cold, so wet-suits are needed. Caution should be used in areas of rocks and strong currents. Surfing may also be enjoyed.

Broken Group Islands

Access to the islands is by boat across open water that is at times rough and dangerous; caution is advised. Most visitors travel to the islands from Banfield, Torquart Bay, Ucluelet and Port Alberni. In summer a 100-passenger cargo vessel carries visitors and small boats between Port Alberni and Gibraltar Island.

Camping: primitive camping areas are located near freshwater supplies on Gilbert, Hand, Willis, Clarke, Benson, Turret and Gibraltar islands. The Broken Group contains four Indian reserves which are not for public use.

Emergency help and information: is available at the warden station in a sheltered bay on the southwest shore of Nettle Island.

Fishing: sea fishing is allowed subject to regulations outlined in British Columbia Tidal Waters Sport Fishing Guide, available at park office and at Federal fisheries offices.

Boating: conditions are good in protected waters, but care is needed in waters studded with reefs often hidden by heavy morning fogs.

West Coast Trail

The trail is not yet incorporated in the park, but visitors may obtain information about weather and trail conditions, routing, and facilities at the park office in the Long Beach section.

Pacific Rim National Park is located 306 km west of Victoria, Vancouver Island; all sections are accessible via Highway 4, which runs west from Parksville and is located off Highway 1, 92 km north of Victoria.

Commercial accommodation and full range of visitors' services are available at either end of the park in the villages of Ucluelet and Tofino.

More information may be obtained from: The Superintendent, Pacific Rim National Park, Box 280, Ucluelet, British Columbia V0R 3A0; telephone (604) 726-7721.

POINT PELEE
Ontario

Point Pelee National Park is unusual in many ways: it is Canada's southernmost point; it enjoys this nation's warmest climate; it is visited by more birds than can be counted; it has two distinctly different frost-free seasons, and it lies at the same latitude as northern California and Spain's Costa Brava, which is on the Mediterranean.

Located on a foundation of glacial sand, silt and gravel that bites into Lake Erie, this spit of land is slightly more than 7 km long by 3.5 km wide at its northern base; its southern extremity is needle-sharp and beset by strong, dangerous currents. During its moist springs, the land produces lush, jungle-like vegetation that gradually dies off to be replaced by desert-type plants during hot, dry spells that arrive in mid-summer, circumstances that allow prickly-pear cactus to grow and blossom during June and July.

Located on two major migration routes, the reserve attracts at least 332 species of birds during spring and again in the autumn, while 90 species nest in the park itself. This twice-yearly invasion of countless numbers of birds attracts a correspondingly large number of bird watchers, who faithfully flock to the park during its two key seasons.

Point Pelee is small in territory, occupying only 15.5 km², two thirds of which are dominated by freshwater marshes, but its location and the variety and numbers of plants and animals found within its perimeters are of considerable significance. As might be expected of a place largely dominated by marsh, the insect population of Point Pelee is also considerable, making it attractive to the birds but rather less so to visitors during the wet season. Compensating for this, however, are the torrid summers, when insects become less and people can enjoy excellent swimming and sunbathing, all the while listening to the songs of a great variety of birds.

Located in a densely populated region, this is a heavily used park. The numbers of visitors flocking to Point Pelee have caused authorities to curtail automobile traffic during the peak summer season, although the car has been replaced by a mini-transit system. Pollution-free, trackless trains carry passengers from the visitor center to the end of the peninsula, called The Tip; en route entertainment is provided by interpretive talks over a public address system. Trains operate from 9 a.m. to 9 p.m. from early April to the end of August and during autumn weekends.

POINT PELEE: THINGS TO DO

Season: year round

Bird watching: is most popular. Facilities for watching and photographing birds are excellent.

Camping: there is no individual camping in the park, but there are two group campgrounds, each having room for 100 people; reservations must be made.

Walking: the Boardwalk Trail extends more than 1 km through the marshland. The Woodland Trail leads through a small, deciduous forest containing elms, basswoods, hackberry, oaks, red ash and silver maples. Other hiking trails are also available; some visitors prefer to walk along the beach.

Swimming: is excellent, with 22 km of beach.

Interpretive programs: are conducted throughout the year and include slide and film shows, talks, displays depicting the park through every season, guided hikes and special programs. A naturalist will meet and speak to individual groups if arrangements are made in advance.

Commercial accommodation and camping in surrounding parks is available.

Access to the park, located 56 km from Windsor, is via Highway 3.

More information can be obtained from: The Superintendent, Point Pelee National Park, R. R. 1, Leamington, Ontario N8H 3V4; telephone: (519) 326-3204.

PRINCE ALBERT
Saskatchewan

Three forms of life characterize Canada's great boreal forests: spruce, moose and cladonia. The first is represented by black and white spruce trees, the second needs no introduction to North Americans, the third is the so-called caribou moss *(Cladonia rangiferina),* a lichen that is two plants in one, for it consists of a partnership between a fungus and an alga. All three are found in Prince Albert National Park, but this reserve's distinguishing characteristics do not end there.

Established in 1927 and encompassing 3875 km² of forest, lakes, streams and wetlands, the gently-rolling land of this reserve in central Saskatchewan shelters a wide variety of other plants and animals and is further distinguished as the resting place of Canada's celebrated writer and conservationist, Grey Owl, who died in 1938 and lies buried on the shores of Lake Ajawaan in the north-central part of the reserve.

Located 200 km north of Saskatoon and reached via Highways 2 and 263, the park is open year round and offers recreational facilities during all seasons. The hub of these activities is found on the shores of Lake Waskesiu, which is also road's end. From here, an enormous expanse of fascinating wilderness awaits those visitors who wish to back-pack or canoe through a land where live some 200 species of birds and a herd of about 20 plains bison that is kept on the reserve; in the forests and clearings are deer, moose, woodland caribou, black bears, timber wolves, lynx and other mammals including, of course, Grey Owl's favorite, the beaver.

Apart from being a mecca for wilderness explorers, Prince Albert has something for everyone. The visitor services center at Waskesiu offers many recreational facilities as well as private overnight accommodation. In addition there is an 18-hole golf course, tennis courts, lawn-bowling greens, a horse-riding stable, a tour boat, movie theaters, a post office, shops, restaurants, service stations and a laundromat.

PRINCE ALBERT: THINGS TO DO

Season: sections of the park are open all year.

Camping: five main campgrounds with facilities varying from fully-serviced to primitive contain a total of 478 sites. In addition small, backcountry campgrounds are located on the shorelines of Crean and Kingsmere Lakes; a group tenting area is available. All backcountry campers must register at the information center before and after each trip.

Interpretive program: includes sunrise hikes, starlight walks, canoe excursions, evening programs, owl hooting, elk bugling, wolf howling and other novel events.

Hiking: day and overnight hikes as well as morning or afternoon strolls give visitors an excellent view of the park. Three major trails are the Kingsmere, the Old Freight and the Kingfisher. While all trails are identified on the folder map obtained at the park entrance, topographic maps can be obtained at the information office or nature center.

Canoeing and boating: the Grey Owl Wilderness and the Bagwa are two popular backcountry trips, but there are several shorter routes and many small and peaceful lakes that are excellent for day trips. Power boats are allowed on Waskesiu, Crean, Kingsmere, Heart and Sandy lakes. Marina facilities are located at Waskesiu and Heart lakes and there is a launching ramp on Sandy Lake.

Fishing: northern pike, walleye perch and lake trout are found in waters on the reserve – the largest trout caught in Saskatchewan was taken from these waters. Fishing licence required.

Winter activities: for five months a year, skiing and snowshoeing enthusiasts enjoy the park, where over 100 km of cross-country skiing and snowshoe trails are maintained. Camping and other overnight accommodation is available.

More information can be obtained from: The Superintendent, Prince Albert National Park, Box 100, Waskesiu Lake, Saskatchewan S0J 2Y0; telephone (306) 663-5322.

PRINCE EDWARD ISLAND
Prince Edward Island

Prince Edward Island, Canada's smallest province, was shaped by ancient accumulations of sand and mud deposited in a large ocean basin. Over the ages, continuing build-ups resulted in the formation of the sandstone which is the base of this island in the Gulf of St. Lawrence. The park named for this province and created in 1937 is contained in a narrow coastal area 18 km² in extent, facing the Gulf, that offers a varied landscape of sand dunes, red sandstone cliffs, marshes, ponds and some of Canada's finest beaches.

The reserve also has a touch of literary history, for at its far, western end is located Green Gables House, the farmhouse that became internationally known as the setting of Lucy Maud Montgomery's classic novel, *Anne of Green Gables.*

Influenced greatly by salt water, the park also has a number of freshwater streams and ponds, nesting sites for ducks such as blue-winged and green-winged teal, ring-necked and black ducks and a variety of shore birds. Great blue herons are also present and have built about 100 nests on Rustico Island, while birds such as the horned lark and a number of sparrows live on the dunes. In all, about 210 species of birds have been seen in this reserve.

The largest mammal in the park is the red fox; in addition, raccoons, skunks, mink, weasel, muskrat, red squirrels and chipmunks inhabit the area.

One of the aspects that most attracts visitors is the swimming. The beaches have fine, red sand constantly smoothed by the ocean and the water is warmer than at many points in the south; at either end of the reserve are Prince Edward Island's gracefully rolling hills, deservedly known as the "Gardens of the Gulf."

PRINCE EDWARD ISLAND: THINGS TO DO

Season: sections of the park are open all year.

Camping: as indicated by more than a million and a half visitors in 1981, the reserve is very popular; it is also the fourth smallest and although there are 569 sites divided into three campgrounds, space is limited and is allocated on a first-come-first-served basis. However, there are guest facilities in adjacent areas, where hotels, motels, tourist homes and private campgrounds may be rented.

Swimming: the fine sands and warm water attract a large number of visitors in July and August. Facilities include changing rooms, showers and canteens located on the major supervised beaches.

Hiking: Bubbling Springs, Reeds and Rushes, Balsam Hollow and other trails allow visitors to see the park at first hand. Beach walking is also popular.

Clam digging: those interested in digging for these shellfish should ask park staff for further information.

Boating: freshwater ponds and lakes are ideal for canoeing and for rowboats; no motors allowed. From many adjacent harbors visitors can arrange to go on deep-sea cruises and fishing trips.

Interpretive programs: are provided year round; summer programs range from guided walks to sand-castle contests. Further information is available at the park.

Winter activities: cross-country skiing, snowshoeing and skating are offered.

Other facilities: include an 18-hole golf course, tennis courts and lawn bowling.

This reserve is located 24 km north of Charlottetown and is accessible via Highways 6 and 15.

More information may be obtained from: The Superintendent,

Prince Edward Island National Park, Box 487, Charlottetown, Prince Edward Island C1A 7L1; telephone (902) 672-2211.

PUKASKWA
Ontario

Skirted by Highway 17 and straddled by the communities of Wawa, White River and Marathon, this park on the shores of Lake Superior was created in 1978, but has not yet been officially opened for public use. It is, however, open to all who would enter it upon the terms of the wilderness – that is to say, only on foot or by canoe can it be explored from the landward side; from lakeside, power boats can reach its shores but from there on, visitors must walk or paddle into the interior.

Pukaskwa (pronounced *púck-a-saw*) National Park will be immediately appealing to those who enjoy getting off the beaten path and who are skilled in the ways of forest and river. The place is full of challenge – an isolated, unspoiled wilderness where black bear and wolf, moose and some woodland caribou and white-tail deer roam the forests and clearings, where the call of the loon is heard often and where other humans are rarely met by the explorer.

Even after its scheduled opening in 1983, this park will retain most of its wildness, for development will be slow, conducted in stages while studies of its geology, ecology and animal life are being made.

Located 626 km north of Sault Ste. Marie, Ontario, Pukaskwa contains 1878 km² of land in a latitude where the Canadian Shield meets the northeast shore of Lake Superior on the southern edge of Ontario's boreal forests. The dominant trees in most of the reserve are black spruce, jack-pine and white birch, but forest types differ with moisture and topography. In the southern section of the reserve are found transition zone trees such as red maple, sugar maple, yellow birch and occasional white pines. Shrubs include mountain maple, red osier, dogwood, blueberry, speckled alder and willow.

Due to the cooling effect of Lake Superior, arctic and alpine plants also grow in the reserve, including saxifrage, northern twayblade and Franklin's ladyslipper. In these habitats roam the many mammals of the region; apart from the large species mentioned, lynx and fox are relatively common, as are beaver, red and flying squirrels and other small animals. About 200 species of birds have been recorded in the park. On some of its small lakes breed such waterfowl as American golden-eyes, black ducks and mergansers; great blue herons nest in rookeries and herring gull colonies are located on the islands adjacent to the western shoreline.

Fish found in park waters include speckled trout, white slicker and lake chub; in Lake Superior live rainbow trout, brown trout, yellow pickerel, lake whitefish, burbot and pink salmon.

Access to the reserve at present is limited to a coastal hiking trail which is open from the Pic River, in the northwest corner of the park at Hattie Cove, and leads south for 68 km to end at Oiseau River. Otherwise, canoers can enter the park from the Pukaskwa River, in the southeast corner and from the White River in the north. Good spring canoeing can be had on the Pukaskwa, while the White offers good canoeing throughout the summer.

A number of primitive campsites are spotted within the reserve.

More information can be obtained from: The Superintendent, Pukaskwa National Park, Box 550, Marathon, Ontario P0T 2T0; telephone (807) 229-0801.

RIDING MOUNTAIN
Manitoba

Riding Mountain National Park contains a varied landscape of evergreen and hardwood forests, prairies, valleys, rolling hills, lakes and streams besides its principal feature, the mountain for which it is named that rises 756 m above sea level.

Located on a rolling plateau that forms part of the Manitoba Escarpment, the park was established in 1929 and contains 2929 km² of land that stands at the crossroads of three habitats. High areas are covered with forests of black and white spruce, jack-pine, balsam fir and tamarack that in places intermingle with stands of aspen and groves of white birch; along the warmer regions following the base of the escarpment, the richer soils support forests of hardwoods as well as shrubs, vines and ferns. In the western part of the reserve, extensive areas are devoted to meadows and grasslands, where a galaxy of wildflowers can be found during June and July.

These blends of vegetation, topography and climate support an almost equally varied number of animals. The home of buffalo before their near extinction, the park was allocated a small herd of these great bovines soon after its creation. Today, some 30 bison roam a partly-forested grassland plain. Black bears and coyotes wander through most sections of the land and moose, elk and white-tail deer inhabit individual ranges best suited to their needs. Beaver are numerous, as are many other, smaller mammals and a variety of birds.

The lakes and rivers of the park contain some record fish. Northern pike are notable for their size and fighting qualities; specimens weighing 13 kilos have been taken in Clear Lake, where walleye perch, whitefish and big lake trout are also found. Katherine and Deep lakes contain rainbow trout.

Riding Mountain National Park is accessible by automobile and bus from the north and the south. Highway 10 connects Brandon, 95 km south, with Wasagaming, where the visitor service center is located. This road continues through the park to Dauphin, 13 km from the reserve's northern boundary.

RIDING MOUNTAIN: THINGS TO DO

Season: sections of the park are open year round.

Camping: campgrounds located in a number of areas range from fully serviced sites to primitive tent pads. Wasagaming Campground has 86 fully-serviced sites for trailer, 72 trailer sites with electricity and 379 unserviced sites; it is equipped with kitchen shelters, toilets and showers. Lake Katherine campground, 5 km from the service center, has 118 campsites without individual services, but toilets and kitchen shelters are centrally located. Near the park's larger lakes are a number of unserviced sites with kitchen shelters, wood-burning stoves and pit privies; all are accessible by car along the highway and park roads. There are two group camping areas: Manito and Kippechewin; facilities include dormitories, a dining hall and fully equipped kitchens. The Wasagaming visitor's center offers a range of hotel, motel and cottage accommodation.

Hiking: a network of hiking and riding trails meanders through the park. A booklet, *Trail Guide,* provides full details and map; it is available at the information center.

Winter activities: include ice fishing in Clear Lake – licence required; cross-country skiing, snowshoeing and downhill skiing at Agassiz Ski Hill.

Swimming/canoeing: visitors will find good swimming in the park;

canoeing and boating waters are excellent and extensive.

Other activities: are varied and include an 18-hole golf course, asphalt-surface tennis courts, lawn bowling, horse and bicycle rentals, and a number of interpretive programs and displays.

More information may be obtained from: The Superintendent, Riding Mountain National Park, Wasagaming, Manitoba R0J 2H0; telephone (204) 848-2811.

ST. LAWRENCE ISLANDS
Ontario

Scattered along 80 km of the St. Lawrence River's Thousand Islands region, this, Canada's smallest national reserve, consists of 4 km² of rocky land distributed among 17 islands and a mainland property at Mallorytown Landing. Established in 1914 and lying between Kingston and Brockville, near the boundary of New York State, the park's territory is composed largely of granite and limestone covered on some islands by thin layers of soil and exposed to the elements on others. Depending on the height above water and governed by the depth and quality of the soil, some of the plants known in the surrounding region are represented in the reserve, including pitch pine, swamp white oak, rue anemone and deerberry.

Large mammals are rare or absent, but a variety of reptiles and amphibians can be observed. The black snake, seldom seen in other parts of Canada, lives on some islands; on others are found ribbon snakes, several kinds of turtles, toads and salamanders. Waterfowl fly over the park during autumn and spring migrations, while species that nest on the mainland visit the islands from time to time; resident on the islands are kingfishers, great blue herons, terns, gallinules, sparrows, wood peewees, warblers and grackles.

Artifacts and debris taken from prehistoric sites suggest that humans inhabited the region some 9000 years ago, probably camping on some of the islands while fishing and hunting. Forming the base of the park and rising from the St. Lawrence River is a ridge of Precambrian granite some 500 million years old that bridges the gap between the Canadian Shield and the Adirondack Mountains of the U.S.A. – a geologic formation known as the Frontenac Axis.

Park headquarters are located at Mallorytown Landing; this and Hill Island are the only sections of the reserve accessible by road, the former via the Thousand Islands Parkway, the latter via the Canadian span on the Thousand Islands International Bridge. All other locations can be reached only by water, but communities and marinas along the parkway offer entrance points to the St. Lawrence.

ST. LAWRENCE ISLANDS: THINGS TO DO

Season: mid-May to mid-October.

Camping: at Mallorytown Landing are 60 sites with water, flush and pit toilets, barbecue pits, fireplaces, firewood, picnic area, beach, changehouse and interpretive exhibits. Most islands have docks, some tent sites, and basic facilities.

Interpretive program: is wide-ranging and includes on-site exhibits, portable displays, audio-visual programs, nature walks and talks.

Other accommodation: the Ontario St. Lawrence Parks Commission operates two serviced campgrounds and a large, day-use area within the surrounding area; these include picnic facilities and a beach. Private accommodation, camping, marinas, boat tours and restaurants are available in the vicinity. Commercial water taxis operate between the mainland and the park islands.

More information can be obtained from: The Superintendent, St. Lawrence Islands National Park, Box 469, R. R. 3, Mallorytown Landing, Ontario K0E 1R0; telephone (613) 923-5241.

TERRA NOVA
Newfoundland

Part of the Appalachian Mountains system, this park is located on Bonavista Bay, on the east coast of Newfoundland. One of its major features is shoreline indented by numerous arms, sounds, coves, inlets, sea caves and rocky headlands. In addition, on the landward side are found a number of shallow bogs and ponds dominated by forests of black spruce that also contain areas where balsam fir, white birch, poplar and mountain ash grow more sparingly.

Terra Nova is Canada's most easterly national park. It was established in 1957 and contains 396 km² of terrestrial-marine landscape situated 250 km northwest of St. John's and 80 km southeast of Gander. This is a region influenced by the Labrador Sea where icebergs are not infrequently sighted in May and June and where summers are cool and winters moderate.

The fierce waters of the North Atlantic pound the coast and travel inland up long inlets, a mix of oceanic and land biology that offers much to interest the nature-oriented visitor. Apart from its forests, Terra Nova has a variety of unusual plants such as wild sarsaparilla, yellow-flowered bluebead lily and stemless ladyslippers; in wet locations grow bog laurel, leatherleaf, pitcher plants, Labrador tea and rarities like Arctic blueberry and curly grass fern.

Native animals include black bear, otter, red fox, lynx and weasel. Moose, mink, squirrels and ruffed grouse are also present, but have been introduced from the mainland. Marine animals are a significant feature of this park. Bay seals, Atlantic white-sided dolphin and humpbacked, pilot, fin and pothead whales are often sighted in the coastal waters adjacent to the park.

Although the park is accessible via the Trans-Canada Highway, mainland visitors must book ferry space to cross to Newfoundland and are advised to make reservations early, as the ferries are congested in summer.

TERRA NOVA: THINGS TO DO

Season: sections of the park are open all year.

Camping: the two main campgrounds, Newman Sound and Alexander Bay, have a total of 600 sites. Facilities include washrooms, playgrounds, individual fireplaces, a restaurant, laundromat, showers and a grocery store. Other primitive campsites are available for hikers, canoeists and boaters.

Interpretive program: outdoor theater presentations during the summer months and four major interpretive themes; details available at park headquarters.

Hiking: is over 80 km of trails, parts of which are open in winter for skiing and snowshoeing.

Other activities: swimming, scuba diving, sailing, boating and an 18-hole golf course are among the varied activities offered.

Fishing: is good in fresh water for trout and salmon – licence required – and there is excellent marine fishing.

More information can be obtained from: The Superintendent, Terra Nova National Park, Glovertown, Newfoundland A0G 2L0; telephone (709) 533-2801.

WATERTON LAKES
Alberta

Tall mountains, undulating prairies and a rich mix of plants and animals are characteristics of the Canadian section of the Waterton-Glacier International Peace Park, which was established in 1932 at the urging of the Rotary Clubs of Alberta and Montana.

Before that, antedating the arrival of Europeans, the Blackfoot Indians held sway in a region of North America that was to remain virtually unknown to all but its native inhabitants until members of the Palliser Expedition explored it in 1858.

Waterton Lakes National Park was first established in 1895 following the discovery of oil in the area, a circumstance that caused a number of local conservationists to petition Ottawa, urging the preservation of at least some of the land in the area of the oil finds. In course of time, the coupling of Waterton with Glacier National Park, Montana, came to pass; today the two reserves jointly contain a section of magnificent wilderness some 104 km long by 56 km wide. The Canadian part is the smaller, occupying a block 21 km long by 25 km wide, for a total of 525 km² of land immediately adjacent to the U.S. border.

Four inter-connected lakes lie in the eastern section of the park. The largest of these is Waterton; it is 12 km long and has a depth of 153 m. It runs through the mountains and enters Montana, ending at Goathaunt Ranger Station, in Glacier. Next is Middle Waterton, followed by Lower Waterton; the smallest and most northerly is Maskinonge. The whole region, however, is well watered. There are many small lakes, rivers and streams on both sides of the border, as a consequence of which the plant life in Waterton Lakes is lush and varied.

Where the mountains meet the prairie a variety of wildflowers grow and bloom in season; among these are wild roses, pasque flowers, wild geranium and double wind flowers; the grasslands support bear berry, silver berry, junipers, saskatoon berries, chokecherries and shrubby cinquefoil. Few trees are found here, but transitional zones between prairie and mountain have clusters of aspens, cottonwoods and Douglas maples.

By far the most numerous trees in the park are evergreens. Up to altitudes of 200 m grow Douglas fir, lodgepole pine, limber pine and, at somewhat lower elevations, white spruce. Higher up are found Engelmann spruce, white bark pine and alpine fir.

Near the timberline, in alpine meadows and on shoulders of mountains live bighorn sheep and mountain goats. Moose, grizzly and black bear usually prefer forested lands that lie at middle elevations, where the red squirrel also makes its home. A small herd of about 20 plains bison have been re-introduced in the park, returning to this ancient habitat a species that almost became extinct in North America at the turn of this century. Elk and mule deer browse in more open forests and in alpine meadows, places dotted with rocky outcrops where the cougar and coyote are also found. In addition to these large animals, the park shelters ground squirrels, marmots, pikas, fox, marten, mink and many other, smaller mammals.

In great, untidy-looking nests high up the slopes, the bald eagle raises its young in habitats it shares with hawks and falcons. During spring and autumn, thousands of migratory ducks and geese stop to rest in Waterton Lakes together with herons, waders, marsh birds and gulls.

WATERTON LAKES: THINGS TO DO

Season: sections of the park are open year round.

Camping: a total of 762 sites are distributed among 19 campgrounds; some of these accommodate only a few people, others, like Townsite and Grandell Mountain, have 240 and 129 sites respectively. Services vary according to location and size. Belly River, Crandell and Townsite can accommodate trailers as well as tents.

Hiking: more than 170 km of trails wind through the mountains and valleys; all are well marked on topographic maps available at the information center. Overnight campers and hikers and anyone traveling off established trails must register in and out with a park warden, or at the administration building. Camping is allowed only at designated backcountry sites.

Fishing: pike, whitefish and several species of trout are caught in the lakes and streams. Licence required.

Swimming: an outdoor, heated pool is located at the townsite and operates during summer.

Boating: canoes and rowboats may be used on most of the larger ponds and lakes in the park. Motorboats may be operated on Waterton Lake.

Interpretive program: offers conducted walks, field trips, fireside talks, auto caravans, slide and film presentations and self-guiding trails. The International, a tour steamer, runs along Waterton Lake, between Waterton National Park and Glacier National Park.

Winter activities: skiing, snowshoeing and snowmobiling are allowed in designated areas.

Other activities: an 18-hole public golf course is located in the park; horses can be rented for riding on some of the park trails.

Waterton Lakes National Park lies 444 km south of Calgary on Highways 2 and 5. It is also accessible from Browning, Montana, along Route 88 and from Columbia Falls, Montana, via the Glacier National Park Highway that connects with Route 88.

More information can be obtained from: The Superintendent, Waterton Lakes National Park, Waterton Park, Alberta T0K 2N0; telephone (403) 859-2262.

WOOD BUFFALO
Alberta-Northwest Territories

Occupying 44807 km² of land, Canada's largest national park straddles the Alberta-Northwest Territories border and contains outstanding examples of the northern boreal wilderness, a territory most of which consists of an enormous, poorly-drained plain underlaid by rock and covered by forests and by a multitude of streams, shallow lakes and bogs.

Established in 1922, the reserve was originally set aside to conserve the last remaining herds of woods bison, but it now offers sanctuary to a number of other important wildlife species, including most of the nesting sites in Alberta of the peregrine falcon, the only known nesting grounds of the endangered whooping crane, the largest free-roaming herd of bison in the world and a variety of animals typical of the boreal forests, such as black bears, wolves, moose, woodland caribou and numbers of smaller aquatic and terrestrial species.

Found within Wood Buffalo National Park are vast salt plains that during dry times form mounds and ridges of salt up to 1.5 m high, the products of evaporation of the heavily-salinated waters of the Salt River. In addition, the reserve safeguards the Peace-Athabasca Delta,

one of the largest freshwater deltas in the world and an important nesting and staging area for many kinds of waterfowl; these waters also support a number of fish populations, the most significant being the goldeye.

The forests of the reserve are composed of jack-pine, spruce, tamarack, aspen and birch, but the trees are frequently interrupted by wet meadows on which grow sedges and grasses and by areas of spongy muskeg, a kind of bog composed of a top layer of sphagnum moss beneath which lie deep sections of decayed vegetation that over many years have been broken down to a rusty-colored mulch that is influenced by permafrost.

Significant landforms include uplands dating from the Cretaceous period 135 million years ago, now known as the Birch and Caribou mountains. Located respectively in the southern and western boundaries of Wood Buffalo, these tablelands rise 420 m above the surrounding plains and are all that now remain of a series of such heights that thousands of years ago covered the region until bulldozed out of existence by massive ice floes.

Below these uplands stretches the Alberta Plateau, the enormous, wet basin that comprises most of the park and in the eastern section of which exist some of the best deposits of gypsum to be found in North America. This soft bedrock is slowly being dissolved by surface water, a circumstance that has created a number of underground rivers, sinkholes and caves. Above ground, the meandering Peace River flows through the southern section and empties into the Slave River after traveling almost 1700 km; the Slave, in its turn, borders the eastern boundary of Wood Buffalo, running north to empty into Great Slave Lake.

Artifacts and fossils in the reserve suggest that the region was originally occupied by man as long as 9000 years ago. During the 18th century, the Alberta section of the park was one of the first areas of the northwest to be explored and settled by Europeans; lured into the wilderness by furs, these early explorers also hoped to discover the fabled, but nonexistent Northwest passage, which was believed to be accessible by means of the Peace River. Fort Chipewyan, which lies just outside Wood Buffalo's eastern boundary, on the shores of Lake Athabasca, was established in 1788. It is the oldest continuously occupied settlement in Alberta. In the early 19th century, the Athabasca, Peace, Slave and Mackenzie rivers became the main transport routes to the north; Fort Fitzgerald and Fort Smith were established and joined Chipewyan as stopping places for those journeying into the wilderness.

Today, apart from the spectacular bison and the rare whooping cranes, the park is famous for the concentration of wildfowl that twice a year visit the Peace-Athabasca Delta. Over a million ducks, geese and swans from four major North American flyways pass through Wood Buffalo in spring and autumn. The northernmost colony of white pelicans nest on the islands of the Slave River near Fort Smith, and a variety of other resident and migratory birds are found throughout the reserve. Mammal and bird lists are available from the park office.

Wood Buffalo is pure wilderness. For this reason, most of its visitor facilities reflect its hinterland flavor. Access is from the south, along Alberta Highway 35 to its junction with Highway 5 in the Northwest Territories, which runs east and west to and from Fort Smith. Visitors from British Columbia can travel via Highway 49 from Dawson Creek, then head north along Highway 2, which joins 35 at Grimshaw. Edmonton, Alberta, lies 1370 km to the south. But whatever the route taken, travelers should be equipped for on-the-road emergencies during off-seasons in a region where distances between communities are long and facilities are limited.

WOOD BUFFALO: THINGS TO DO

Season: sections of the park are open all year.

Camping: there is a 36-site campground, picnic site and group camp at Pine Lake, 66 km south of Fort Smith; reservations must be made for the group camp. At Klewi Lake, off Highway 5, there is a wayside stop with dock, outhouse and picnic facilities. A primitive, overnight campground is located at Rainbow Lake. Tenting and other primitive camping is allowed anywhere in the park as long as the site is 1.5 km distant from Pine Lake and from any road or trail. These backcountry trips require registration in and out. The Government of the Northwest Territories maintains a campsite and picnic area at Little Buffalo Falls, just outside the park's northwestern boundary, and another at Fort Smith. There is also a campground and picnic site at Thebacha, 30 km north of Fort Smith. Hotels are available at Fort Smith and Fort Chipewyan.

Hiking: trails for hiking, cross-country skiing and snowshoeing are numerous and scenic; a number of these have been developed to pass through particularly interesting country. Up-to-date trail guides are available from the park office.

Interpretive programs: naturalists offer regular evening talks, hikes, and other activities, including buffalo "creeps," when visitors can be guided to a safe distance from grazing bison.

Boating: the rivers in the region are usually slow-flowing and muddy; the Delta is difficult to navigate, and the large lakes can be extremely dangerous because of sudden and fierce squalls. It is good practice to check conditions and register at the park office before undertaking a trip. Under permit, motorboats may be used on Pine Lake, the Peace, Athabasca and Slave Rivers and the delta channels connecting Lake Athabasca to the Peace and Slave Rivers.

Fishing: pike, pickerel, whitefish, suckers and inconnu, a large, northern species that may weigh up to 28 kilos, are the most common fish found in park waters; licence required.

More information can be obtained from: The Superintendent, Wood Buffalo National Park, Box 750, Fort Smith, Northwest Territories X0E 0P0; telephone (403) 872–2349.

(See also the Introduction, especially for more information on the bison and whooping cranes.)

YOHO
British Columbia

In 1858, while members of Captain John Palliser's expedition were exploring the western mountains, a packhorse kicked Dr. James Hector, one of the explorers, as the group was making its way through a steep declivity. This baulky animal was thus responsible for naming Kicking Horse Pass, an opening in the Rockies with its entrance on the borders of Alberta and British Columbia.

In 1884, when the Canadian Pacific Railway laid track through the pass, reports filtering back to Ottawa regarding the beauty and accessibility of the surrounding country caused the federal government to set aside 16 km² of land as a reserve: Yoho National Park was created two years later, in 1886.

In 1930, the boundaries of the park were set at 1313 km² and Yoho today forms the northwestern section of what is known as The Four

Mountain Park Block, the other three reserves being Jasper and Banff in Alberta and Kootenay, which lies immediately south of Yoho, in British Columbia.

During the many thousands of years that have elapsed since the Rocky Mountains were formed, ice, wind, rain, snow and cold have combined to further embellish the sedimentary – and therefore easily eroded – rocks, the results of all this scouring being seen today in the steep canyons, deep river valleys, and the Hoodoos, those strange formations that stand as though sculpted into abstract figures by human agency.

Animals and plants are well adapted to the country and have flourished in areas and ranges best suited to their needs and in accordance with the seasons. Three different biological zones have been identified in this reserve, each giving rise to its own populations of plants and animals, but none separated by distinct topographic lines. Instead, one zone leads gradually into another, creating transition areas where species intermingle. The lower, montane region is distinguished by grassy meadows and forests of Douglas fir, white spruce and lodgepole pine; above this, in the sub-alpine region, grow Engelmann spruce and alpine fir as well as lodgepole pine. These two ranges are occupied at different seasons by moose, deer, elk, black bear, cougar and mountain goats, a variety of smaller mammals, and many species of birds. The highest land in the reserve, the alpine region, is occupied by mountain goats, grizzly bears, marmots and pikas in addition to lesser animals and birds. Plants here have had to adapt to a short growing season and to more severe weather conditions; few trees of any stature exist, but wildflowers and shrubby plants are numerous.

Because of the presence of many gentle valleys, Yoho is particularly suited to foot travel; this is, in fact, the best way to see and to understand the wonders contained by this exceptional reserve.

YOHO: THINGS TO DO

Season: year round, with facilities restricted in winter.
Camping: five campgrounds in the park contain more than 300 sites. Kicking Horse, Hoodoo Creek and Chancellor Peak can accommodate trailers as well as tents.

Tents only are allowed at Takakkaw Falls and Lake O'Hara campgrounds.
Hiking: backcountry trails wind through many and varied kinds of terrain. All are well marked and topographic maps are available at the administration office in Field, or at the information bureau, where an additional publication dealing with the trails may also be obtained. Overnight hikers, climbers and anyone traveling off established trails must register at one of the reserve's self-registration stations.
Riding: horses may be rented at Emerald Lake but riding is restricted in some areas; visitors should check with the information bureau for details.
Fishing: Dolly Varden char and many kinds of trout are found in the lakes and streams. Best fishing results in waters that are not clouded by silt. Licence required.
Boating: powerboats cannot be used in any area of the park. Canoes and rowboats can be operated on most of the larger ponds and lakes.
Winter activities: cross-country ski-touring is a popular winter activity; all skiers must register in and out at self-registration stations. Many backcountry trails are available for winter use, but skiers should check with park wardens for trail conditions and avalanche hazards before setting out. Snowshoeing is also permitted; the same regulations apply. Snowmobiles are allowed in the park only on designated trails, but permits must be obtained for their use at the operations center. All other motorized vehicles are confined to public roads.
Interpretive program: consists of guided walks, evening fireside gatherings, campground theater slide talks, self-guiding trails and informative publications. A program of events is available at the information bureau and at campground kiosks. Organized groups are invited to use the service during the off-season, but should make arrangements in advance with the park naturalist.

The park is accessible from the east via Highway 93 in Banff and from the west via the Trans-Canada Highway; the eastern entrance is 93 km northwest of the Banff townsite; the western entrance is 49 km east of Golden, British Columbia.

More information can be obtained from: The Superintendent, Yoho National Park, Box 99, Field, British Columbia V0A 1G0; telephone (604) 343-6324.

(See also Banff, Jasper and Kootenay national parks.)

AUYUITTUQ

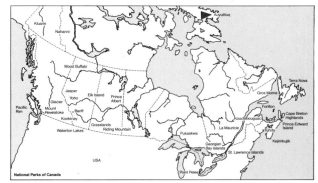

Auyuittuq is a unique arctic wilderness of perpetual ice, mountain peaks and deep valleys on Baffin Island, in Canada's far north.

The need for a quiet, natural, challenging place is common to many people living in the modern world, and this is what draws visitors from all over the world to Auyuittuq.

Above: an emergency cabin at the base of Overlord Peak, Pangnirtung Pass.

Top right: hiking in Weasel River Valley.

Right: a break, simply to wonder at the scenery, during a hike.

Facing page: Glacier hiking at the summit of Pangnirtung Pass, with flat-topped Mount Asgard in the distance.

BANFF

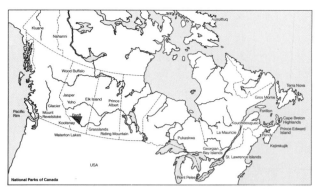

Two views in Banff, the oldest of Canada's national parks.
Left: **Peyto Lake from Lookout Point and** *above* **Lower Waterfowl Lake with Mount Chephren in the background.**

The early light of dawn in Banff National Park as Bow Lake is seen *above* with Portal Peak, Bow Glacier and Mount Thompson in the background. At the other end of the day Mount Rundle *facing page* is reflected in the waters of Vermilion Lake.

Early-morning sunlight on Lake Louise *left and right* **with Victoria Glacier in the background.** *Top:* **Banff Avenue seen from the gardens of the park administration building with Cascade Mountain beyond. St. Nicholas Peak stands high behind the Crowfoot Glacier** *above.*

Above: **glacial landscapes, lakes, mountains and clear, clean air all contribute to the magic of Banff National Park.** *Facing page:* **fresh snow covers the land at Banff's Big Beehive.**

CAPE BRETON HIGHLANDS

The western shore of Cape Breton Highlands National Park, *left,* looking towards Chéticamp from French Mountain Lookout.
The Cabot Trail – seen *above* as it leads from the Western Shore to French Mountain – takes the traveler right onto the plateau, offering a glimpse of some of the last remaining wilderness in the area.

Facing page: **the delightful Corner Brook, on the trail to Corner Brook Falls.**
Top left: **on the eastern coast, the view towards Middle Head from the Franey Tower Lookout Point, and** *top right,* **the Atlantic meeting the coast at Green Cove.** *Above:* **the cliffs and beach at Rocky Bay, north of Broad Cove and** *bottom left,* **looking south along the western shore towards Chéticamp from near Les Grands Falaises.**

ELK ISLAND

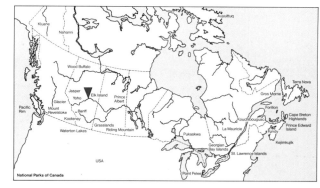

Frost crisps the grasses and reeds, and early-morning mist
drifts over the surface of **Astotin Lake** *left and above.*

A delicate tracery of trees and grasses silhouetted against the evening sky over Astotin Lake.

Elk Island is a virtual oasis of wilderness in a region dominated by man's civilization. The moods, as seen in these pages, can change rapidly, from misted landscape to glowing sunlight.

From near 'The Point' dawn sets the sky alight with its golds and pinks *far right* across Astotin Lake while *right and bottom right* the setting sun lays its path on the lake's waters and trembling aspens are reflected in its surface *facing page.*

Below: Canada geese stand on newly formed ice on Astotin Lake.

In addition to the commoner plains bison *bottom right* **rare woods bison** *below, bottom and facing page* **are kept in a separate enclosure south of Highway 16 in Elk Island National Park.**

The bull elk and his harem of cows *right* stand in an aspen-bordered glen. Autumn is the rutting, or breeding season for these large members of the deer family.

The bones of a long-dead elk, *top left,* lie in the snow while a muskrat, *top right,* perches on a tree by the water's edge. Trembling aspens reach into the light, *top center,* and fallen trees lie at the eastern boundary of the park *above and above right. Facing page:* snow-spattered trees in the boreal forest in the park's woods bison area.

FORILLON

Like a bridal veil, a stream spills its waters over a rock ledge *above* on the La Chute trail. *Left:* flowers of the Arctic Alpine saxifrage.

The massive, tilted block that forms Forillon contains ten different geological formations dating from the Ordivician to the Devonian period. The pictures on these pages all show varying features of Cap Gaspé with Cap Bon Ami *top right*.

FUNDY

Surrounded by thick forestation, the quiet roadside pond *left* **lies near Kinnie Brook, while** *above* **is the energetically-rushing water of Dickson Falls after heavy rain.**

Over 200 species of birds are recorded in Fundy, including the magnificent peregrine falcon *above*. Rising and falling twice each day, the Bay of Fundy's tides are among the highest in the world. Low tide exposes the mud of the Upper Salmon River *top right* and Alma's Beach *far right. Right* is the covered bridge over the Forty-Five River and *facing page* Point Wolfe Dam and the covered bridge over the Point Wolfe River.

GEORGIAN BAY ISLANDS

The sun filters through the overhanging branches and foliage to create a lovely woodland scene *left* **on Beausoleil Island, the largest in the system.** *Above:* **the scene at Finger Point.**

Top left: **the view from Castle Bluff along the north shore of Flowerpot Island. Above Castle Bluff are the caves and rock formations** *top right. Left:* **"Large Flowerpot" on Flowerpot Island, where the bunchberry** *above* **and the one-leaf rein orchis** *top center* **are also found.** *Facing page:* **the quiet, leaf-covered trail through the woods, near Castle Bluff, Flowerpot Island.**

GLACIER

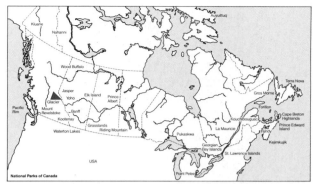

Glacier National Park is located in one of the most rugged areas of Western Canada – the Selkirk Mountains. *Left* is the view from Alpine Meadow, on Abbott Ridge, looking towards the Asulkan Glacier and Dome Point.
　　Above: Rogers Pass and the Hermit Range, from Abbott Ridge Trail.

Black bears come in shades that range from black to brown and cinnamon; *right*, this one, a deep cinnamon, has just finished eating leftovers from a plate. Feeding bears and other animals in all of Canada's national parks is strictly forbidden! *(Photograph: Parks Canada).*

The falls *below* are fed by melt waters of the Vaux Glacier (at top of picture) hanging from the slopes of Mount Macdonald.

Spruce trees, Lookout Mountain and the Asulkan Glacier seen from Glacier Crest, *below far right.*

Facing page: **Clouds move through an alpine valley on the slopes of Mount Macdonald.**

Left: **A hoary marmot takes his ease in Illecillewaet Campground.** *(Photograph: Parks Canada – John G. Woods).*

Below: **Western anemone and** *bottom* **bunchberries on the path to Mount Macdonald.** *(Anemone photograph: Parks Canada – J. Belisle).*

The foaming waters of Bear Falls, on Connaught Creek *right* **and,** *facing page,* **Mount Afton at sunset, seen from Glacier Crest.**

GRASSLANDS

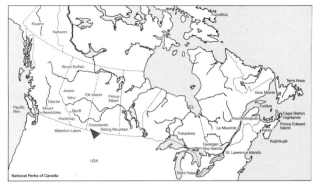

A gravel road in Grasslands, *left,* in the grip of early winter snow. *Above:* the folded landscape of the prairie seen from Lookout Point.

Prairie dogs in the vastness of the prairie, at Dogtown, near Lookout Point *below and top right.*
 Telephone cables line the margin of a snow-sprinkled dirt road *center.*
 Bottom pictures: snow lies patchily on the Killdeer Badlands, seen from Seventy Mile Butte, and storm clouds gather over the prairie landscape, *facing page.*

GROS MORNE

Gros Morne, located on the west coast of Newfoundland's
Great Northern Peninsula, contains some of Canada's most
geologically interesting and spectacular land forms. *Left:*
the cliffs of Green Gardens from Lobster Cove and *above,*
Western Brook Pond.

Below: **the might of Bakers Brook Falls seen from the air.** *Right:* **the boardwalk and** *facing page* **the wind-rippled surface of one of the ponds on the trail to Western Brook Pond. The remaining pictures show three different aspects of the cliffs and coastline at Green Gardens.**

The view *left* towards Lobster Cove Head Lighthouse – just visible behind the trees at left center – with Green Gardens in the distance. *Above:* horses enjoying the tidal pools on the beach in St. Paul's Bay.

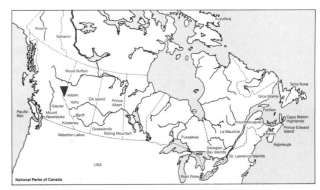

Waters reflect the blue of the sky and the colors of the clouds at Medicine Lake *above* **and Maligne Lake** *left.*

The Athabasca Glacier *these pages* lies at the southern end of Jasper National Park, near the Icefield Center. The center offers information, slide shows and guided walks with park naturalists.

Clouds almost obscure Mushroom Peak and the Athabasca Valley *facing page*, **and Tangle Ridge** *top left* **across the Sunwapta River from Icefields Parkway.** *Above right:* **dawn breaks on the Athabasca and Dome glaciers seen from Wilcox Pass.** *Top right:* **the Athabasca River and Valley, near Jasper, and** *above left* **mountain goats at Disaster Point mineral salt lick.**

Huge rocks mimic the shapes of the Opal Hills behind
Medicine Lake, seen at dawn *right*. Angel Glacier, on the
slopes of Mount Edith Cavell, just catches the first rays of
morning sunlight *above*.

Water runs off the rocks *left,* **of Maligne Canyon to join the rushing Maligne River.** *Above:* **Maligne Lake offers many and varied vistas to the explorer.**

KEJIMKUJIK

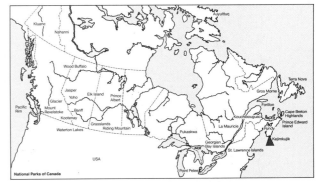

Most of the park's waters are dark brown in color, stained by the bogs they flow through. The rich forestation lining the banks of rivers is deceptive: almost the entire area has been burned or logged within the last 200 years. *Left:* Mill Falls on the Mersey River *above.*

Waterways are the essence of Kejimkujik. The lake of the same name is one of the largest in the province, and unequaled for canoeing. These woods and rivers were the seasonal home of the nomadic Micmac Indians for hundreds of years before the first Europeans came to Canada. Where the trees overhang the still waters, a special kind of peace is created. *Left, bottom left and far left:* participants in an interpretation paddle in the evening on the Mersey River. *Top left:* canoeists near Jake's Landing, and *below* children enjoying Kejimkujik Lake, at Kedge Beach.

Hardly a ripple disturbs the waters of Kejimkujik Lake *above* save for the gentle wake of a slow-moving canoe. *Top left:* pickerel weed at the edge of the Mersey River. *Left and far left:* Kejimkujik Lake pictured near Merrymakedge. *Facing page:* trees overhang a quiet stretch of the Mersey River.

White-tail deer *right, bottom right and facing page;* **the uncomfortable-looking porcupine** *far right and bottom left* **and the spruce grouse** *below* **form a small sample of the wildlife that inhabits or visits Kejimkujik.**

A canoe *facing page* breaks the reflections in the waters of the Mersey River in the late evening light.

Floating heart plants pattern the water of Kejimkujik Lake *top right* as does the extensive growth of water lilies *bottom left.*

Nectar is sipped from a Rosepogonia orchid *bottom right* while *top left* is an example of the rare coastal plain plant, meadow beauty.

KLUANE

Clouds fill the sky, *left,* **above Kluane's St. Elias Mountain Range.**
Above: **the sun sets beyond the far shore of Kathleen Lake.**

The eroded face of Kluane's Goat Mountain *above* viewed from St. Elias Lake. *Facing page:* the deep blue of the evening sky is seen in the waters of a tributary feeding St. Elias Lake.

Red Castle Ridge *top left and left* lit by the early morning sun and *above* shrouded in cloud, from Sheep Bullion Plateau. Also from the plateau may be seen the peaks of the Vulcan Mountain Ranges *far left*.

Glacial Hummock Lake *facing page* at the toe of the Kaskawulsh Glacier, on the Kaskawulsh Glacier floor.

The panorama *above* shows the Slims River from Mount Vulcan Sub Alpine Plateau with the Kluane Range in the background. Frost-sculptured rocks *facing page* on Mount Vulcan, with the Kaskawulsh Valley Glacier forcing its inexorable way as it carves the floor of the valley.

Gribble Gulch *right* is a small stream fed by glacial run-off from the St. Elias Mountains, seen in the background.

Glacial ice *far right* litters the shore of a hummock lake at the terminal of the Kaskawulsh glacier with, in the background, Mount Vulcan.

Below: a sweeping panorama of the Alsek Valley at sunset.

Bottom right: the upper peaks of the Kaskawulsh Mountain Ranges seen from the Mount Vulcan Sub-Alpine Plateau.

Facing page: Mount Maxwell, the highest peak of the Kaskawulsh ranges, lit by the midsummer evening sun.

133

KOOTENAY

Left: a view of Vermilion Fire Burn showing the dead trees that resulted after a forest fire ravaged the area. All visitors to the national parks are urged to be careful with fires. *Above*, a close-up of the same burn on the slopes of Stanley Peak.

Mount Harkin, *left,* **is seen here surrounded by neighboring peaks, their snowy heads reflected in waters painted by sky colors.** *Above,* **a view of the same mountains taken from a different angle.**

Facing page: **a bull moose in the lower stretches of the Vermilion Fire Burn;** *below,* **a watchful coyote.** *Left* **is shown the view from McLeod Meadows looking across the Kootenay River. The potholes** *bottom left* **were carved by the waters of the Vermilion River.** *Bottom,* **a scene at the treeline, near Stanley Glacier.**

KOUCHIBOUGUAC

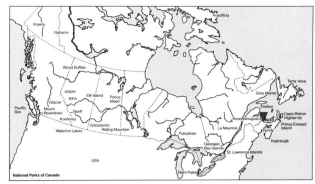

These aerial views of Kouchibouguac show very clearly the dunes, north of Kelly's Beach, *above* **and Kelly's Beach and the extensive boardwalk** *left.*

Left: **Tern Island and the southern end of Kelly's Beach seen from the air. On the Kouchibouguac River, near the boat house, the late afternoon sun** *below* **gives way to a golden sunset** *bottom left and facing page,* **where canoeists take advantage of the last moments of daylight to create a timeless scene. Snaking through the lush vegetation is Kelly's Bog Trail,** *bottom right.*

Common terns fill the sky, *facing page,* above Tern Island. *Top, far right:* the somewhat untidy-looking nest of the common tern, complete with three eggs. *Bottom left:* a tern chick 'plays dead', lying still and quiet in an attempt to avoid its enemies' interest. The osprey *bottom right* nests in the park and has become its symbol. Park wardens *top left* on boat patrol in St. Louis Bay. *Top center:* a stranded jellyfish at the edge of Kelly's Beach.

144

LA MAURICIE

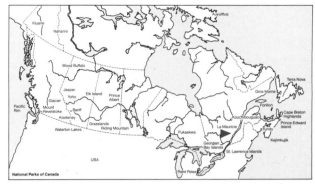

Canoeists *left* paddle the peaceful waters at the southern end of Lake Wapizagonke and *above*, a riot of autumn colors blanket the slopes at Lac à Saur.

La Mauricie offers beautiful beaches for swimming and surfing such as at Lake Edouard *below* and Lac à la Pêche *bottom right,* from where the park warden is seen going about his duties.

There is no doubt that canoeing *right and facing page* and canoe camping are among the most popular activities.

All the seasons have their attractions and winter transforms the park into a different world. There is little doubt, however, that most people would find the glorious colors of fall, *these pages*, breathtakingly beautiful.

A lazy sky softens and transforms the landscape seen from
Le Passage lookout, *left.* Burnished reds and yellows of
early autumn splash fire among the greens of trees at Lac à
Sam, *top.* Some aspects of the park such as the location of
the waterfall *above* are not publicized because of the
fragility of the environment. *Right:* true wilderness – Lac en
Croix Brook.

Reflections of grasses and rocks in the mirror-like waters of Alphonse Lake *above*. At this point Caribou Brook *right* lies almost hidden by the thick vegetation on all sides.

MOUNT REVELSTOKE

Winding its way through the forest *left* **is the boardwalk of Mount Revelstoke's Giant Cedars Trail, where growths of devil's club** *above* **here display autumnal shades.**

Facing page: While sundown casts a purple glow over the land, the full moon emerges above the mountains, a common sight in a region where the sun is early hidden by the peaks. Ice Box Gorge, *right,* and the Revelstoke Mountains in the background.

Fall colours surround the bright red berries of a mountain ash, *below,* pictured on the Eva and Miller Lakes Trail. *Bottom right:* Eva Lake and Mount Williamson Ridge.

NAHANNI

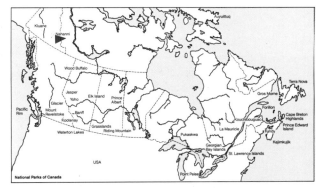

The glancing rays of the setting sun highlight clumps of cottongrass *left* **on the floor of Prairie Creek. The heavy smoke of a forest fire almost obscures Nahanni Butte Mountains in the background** *above.*

A forest fire *facing page* on the border of Nahanni Park. Not necessarily as destructive as they may appear, fires can play an important part in the ecology of the forest. The Sluice Box Rapids System *bottom left* lies immediately before Virginia Falls, seen *top left* with characteristic mid-morning rainbow and *top right* at "night": this region has long periods of daylight in summer. *Above:* an army campsite downriver from Virginia Falls.

162

Facing page: **canoes and rafts at rest beneath the towering face of the aptly-named Pulpit Rock.**

Supplies being unloaded *top left* **from a Sea Otter floatplane near Virginia Falls in preparation for a raft trip** *bottom left and right* **to Nahanni Butte Indian Settlement. A rainbow** *above* **across the foot of Virginia Falls.**

On the Nahanni River, rafts encountering white water *right* at Rafferty's Riffle, First Canyon, and *below left* in Second Canyon. A peaceful river and wooded mountain slopes *bottom right* form an idyllic setting at the entrance to Deadmen Valley. *Facing page:* rafts leaving Third Canyon, immediately before Morengo Creek.

Canoers and rafters seen on these pages note the smoke that is shrouding the area around First Canyon as the forest continues to burn.

PACIFIC RIM

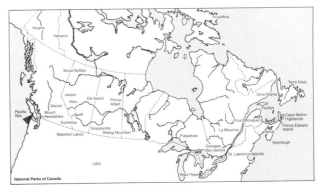

The glory of sunset across the gently rolling sea at Green Point *above* and at Long Beach *left* creates scenes in Pacific Rim National Park that are as timeless as the setting sun itself.

Purples and violets of the dawn reflected *above* in a tidal pool at Pacific Rim's Schooner Cove.
Facing page: the twisted and gnarled stump of a dead cedar at Grice Bay.

Driftwood on the rocks at dawn, South Beach *above* **and at sunset** *facing page.*

A characteristic of all coastal areas in Canada is the tide and the influence it has on shoreline life. Here, *above*, low tide uncovers a variety of small organisms. *Facing page:* gulls are tidal feeders, seen here hunting for small fish.

Sea anemones *above* **lying in a shallow tidal pool at Pacific Rim's Cox Point and** *facing page* **sculpted headlands at Chesterman Beach.**

The incoming sea temporarily reclaims the rocks and tidal pools of a small pocket beach *above* near Sealion Rocks on the West Coast Trail.

From Clarke Island, looking through the Broken Group Islands *right* towards the Vancouver Island coastline.

Western red cedars and amabalis firs are shown *top right,* seen from the Rain Forest Trail.

Facing page: the southernmost point of Broken Group Islands, with Vancouver Island in the background.

At sundown, the land and the sea change, as shown by the tidal pool photographed during early morning, on page 172, and the same scene taken just before sunset, *above.*
Facing page: moisture is a dominant influence on the west coast of Canada; mist often shrouds the land and the water, rising slowly on still days and putting down a milky fog on the sea and distant shores; here, at Sealion Rocks.

A fishing boat, *left*, runs through the fog-shrouded waters of the Broken Group Islands. *Below*, a view of Ucluelet harbor. *Right*, bald eagles constantly scan the waters for fish, the main prey of these great birds. *Bottom, left and right*, a female killer whale seen soon after it has risen, blown and taken a new breath. *Center*, a beacon light on Broken Group Islands.

POINT PELEE

Point Pelee is Canada's southernmost region. Seen from the air above Lake Erie is Red Head Pond *above* **and some of the many species of trees found in the park** *left.*

Above: **sunset over Point Pelee's changeable marshland** *facing page.* **Under the canopy of the trees** *top center* **and in the dunes and open meadows,** *right and top left,* **wild flowers grow profusely; poppies and wild puccoon are among the species to be found.** *Top right:* **a splintered and weathered tree root on East Beach.**

Driftwood, seagulls and fishermen gather at Point Pelee, its tip pointing across the waters to the United States, far over the horizon, *these pages.*

Point Pelee is a living museum of natural history which contains many and varied species of plant and animal life such as the Canada anemones, *bottom left*, **the painted turtle** *far right* **and Blanding's turtle** *bottom right and facing page*, **some of which can at times be observed from the boardwalk** *below*.

PRINCE ALBERT

Morning light on the Waskesiu River and *left* **a roadside pond near the Heart Lakes in Saskatchewan's Prince Albert National Park.**

Right: **a beaver lodge on Amiskowan Lake and** *far right* **the view from the Shady Lake lookout.** *Below:* **towards Shady Lake from "Height-of-Land" firetower.** *Bottom right* **is a creek leading from Shady Lake to Amiskowan Lake.** *Facing page:* **the fury of an electrical storm as it passes over Halkett Lake.**

Cattails growing in a creek *above* leading from Shady Lake
to Amiskowan Lake. *Facing page:* a beaver lodge
constructed at the edge of Amiskowan Lake.

Better photographs than these of a beaver at work would be hard to come by. It should be noted that although the beaver cuts through a lot of wood, it only eats the bark of the trees that it downs. In

middle picture, *left*, the beaver pauses for a snack of newly-cut poplar bark – which tastes rather like cucumber.

Late evening across South Bay *above* and looking towards
King Island *facing page*, on Waskesiu Lake.

Above, a fiery sky over the trees lining the shore of
Waskesiu Lake and *right* Waskesiu River just after dawn.

Top left, **a red squirrel;** *above:* **the great horned owl;** *top center and facing page:* **plains bison** *(Bison bison); top right:* **barred owl and** *right:* **white-tail deer.**

The Kingsmere River *above right* carries its water to the sandy-shored Kingsmere Lake *above left*. Reflections of trees in a roadside pond *top left* near the Heart Lakes, and Ajawaan Lake *top right* on the shores of which stands Grey Owl's cabin, *facing page*, where he did much of his writing.

The view, *left,* shows the extent of wooded land within the park, photographed from Boundary Fire Tower. *Above:* first-growth aspen leave room within their ranks for profuse shrubs and flowers while at right, the aspen have closed ranks, allowing little light to reach the forest floor. The spruces in the lower background have, however, managed to gain a foothold in the aspen domain.

PRINCE EDWARD ISLAND

The easily-eroded red sandstone cliffs of Prince Edward Island are readily apparent in the view *left* towards Orby Head. Further along the shore the sandstone gives way to shore *above* at Rustico Beach.

Under the influence of storm waves and winds, barrier islands formed by the breaking down of sandstone rubble migrate shorewards, resulting in the extensive beaches such as Ross Lane Beach *right and below.* The beach sand is then driven further inshore by wind action and trapped by marram grass, resulting in the formation of the coastal dunes.

Facing page: the Stanhope Cape lighthouse stands starkly white against the clear blue sky. The "Dalvay-by-the-Sea" hotel is shown *bottom right* in its setting by Dalvay Lake.

Broken red sandstone rubble litters the shore *far left* near Orby Head and *left* near Cavendish.

Dwarfed by the rocks on which they stand and the incoming waves, two cormorants *below* pictured at Orby Head, where the sun casts its strong glare across the sea *bottom left. Right:* some of the island's many species of grasses and wild flowers, here seen on the clifftop at Cape Turner.

Vacationers *facing page* **make full use of the fine weather and the facilities of Cavendish Main Beach.**

How fine the balance between existence and extinction of so many species of wildlife and how necessary our awareness of it: this is something about which the park services constantly strive to inform people. An example of an endangered species is the piping plover, *this page,* defending its chick and egg on Cavendish Sandspit.

The huge ball of the sun appears to rest delicately on the horizon *left* at sunset from Cavendish Beach *below*. Just along the coast from Cavendish Beach the waves eat inexorably at the soft red sandstone *bottom*.

Green Gables House *facing page* is located at the western end of the park in Cavendish. This lovely farmhouse is known to millions of readers through Lucy Maud Montgomery's classic novel, *Anne of Green Gables*.

PUKASKWA

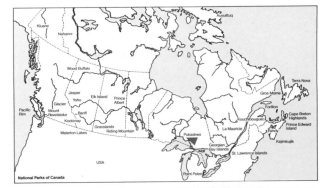

"A Wild Shore on an Inland Sea." The 'wild shore' is the Canadian Shield and the 'inland sea' is Superior – the largest of the Great Lakes. It is these factors that give Pukaskwa – pronounced Púk-a-saw – its wild fascination.

"Superior is a sea: she breeds storms and rain and fog like the sea . . . She is wild, masterful and dreaded." The Reverend George Grant's words are all too apparent when viewing the storm-tossed debris hurled on the shores of Lake Superior *these pages* following a storm.

Pukaskwa National Park, on the shores of Lake Superior, has been described as having 'wild, awesome and fascinating appeal'. In this wilderness live, in addition to the black bear *left*, moose, wolf, woodland caribou and many other, smaller animals.

Far left and below right is a quiet creek at the head of Hattie Cove, on the Coastal Hiking Trail; *bottom left* is the cove's shoreline while *facing page* is the oddly-named Onion Island, also in Hattie Cove.

Above: a scene in the Boreal Forest – which contains spruce, fir, birch, poplar, jack pine, tamarack and aspen – on Southern Headland. *Facing page:* the evening sky streaked with gold and violet across Horseshoe Beach towards Superior's Pic Island and Ogilvy Point.

RIDING MOUNTAIN

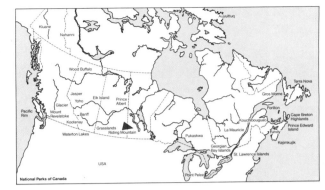

These pages: **the road to Lake Audy makes its way through pure stands of trembling aspen and balsam poplars, the leaves of the trees gold in the early morning sun.**

The reds, yellows and golds of fall at Ominnik Marsh *above* contrast with the ominous build-up of heavy storm clouds over Clear Lake, *facing page.*

Autumn leaves *left and above* gather at the water's edge along Dead Ox Creek on the 'Burls and Bittersweet' trail. A snowshoe hare, *above right*, attempts to blend with the surrounding vegetation.

Frosted undergrowth *bottom* by a beaver pond in the west of Riding Mountain Park. The plains buffalo *below* should feel at home here as skeletal remains indicate that herds once roamed the area. *Right:* 'The Bench' above Birdtail Valley with discarded elk antlers in the foreground. *Facing page:* on the highland plateau, near Highway 10.

ST. LAWRENCE ISLANDS

Magnificently gnarled and convoluted roots of a pine, *left,* **force their way through and around the rocks at the water's edge on Endymion Island.** *Above:* **the shaded floor of a forest on Hill Island.**

Above and top left: **the Thousand Islands/Ivy Lea Bridge crossing over Georgina and Constance Islands, from Hill Island.** *Top, facing page and above left:* **aerial shots of some of the richly-forested islands in the St. Lawrence River that make up this remarkable national park.**

Great blue herons nesting in the St. Lawrence Islands National Park. The great blue is the largest of the heron family and wades in shallow water, catching fish and water animals with a swift jab of its bill.

Rocks thrust from the ground on Mermaid Island like jumbled gravestones in a country churchyard and beech maples almost meet overhead in a forest on Hill Island, *facing page. Far left:* hairy beardtongue on West Grenadier Island and a wood lily puts out its flower. Dearberries on West Grenadier Island, *below.*

Boats moored *below* at the landing stage on Georgina Island with the Ivy Lea Bridge soaring overhead in the background and at night mooring on Camelot Island, *bottom right.*
   Bottom left: a night view of the 'National Parks Showboat' at Mermaid Island and *left* part of the island's rocky coastline. *Bottom center* is Halfmoon Bay, on Bostwick Island and *right,* wind-blown white pines are silhouetted against the cloud-filled sky.

TERRA NOVA

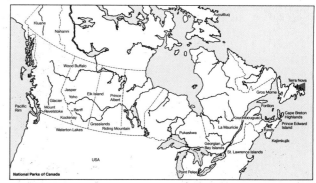

National Parks of Canada

A crescent moon hangs over the trees of a forest *left* near Big Brook, and the setting sun catches highlights on the waves in Newman Sound *above*.

Carnivorous plants do not devour their prey by chewing but, after trapping insects, they subject them to the decomposing actions of digestive enzymes, bacteria or both. Most carnivorous species are green plants that manufacture food in the normal way by photosynthesis from the raw materials of sunlight, water and carbon dioxide in the presence of chlorophyll, and they are not, therefore, sustained by the animal diet alone. *Above:* the pitcher plant, the flower emblem of Newfoundland, and *facing page,* the sundew plant.
   Above right: **Ochre Hill Pond** and *right,* **cladonia lichen ('British soldiers').**

Far left: rock formations, and *left,* fishermen bringing home their catch, in Newman Sound.

Moonrise *bottom left* over the Terra Nova landscape.

Rocks on the shores of Salton's Brook Cove highlighted by the evening sun *below* and, *facing page,* a beaver pond at Burnt Point.

WATERTON LAKES

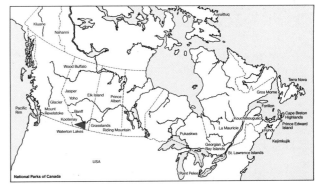

National Parks of Canada

In a timeless scene *left* buffalo graze the prairie in Waterton Lakes
National Park. A view *above* of the prairie land rolling towards the
Waterton Lakes Mountains.

255

The snow-dusted Livingstone Mountains rise sheer behind Cameron Lake *top left* while snow covers the shoreline of Summit Lake *left*. The scene *above* shows the weathered roots of a dead spruce with Vimy Ridge in the background behind Upper Waterton Lake.

The stunning view *right* is of Blakiston Valley from the Mount Crandell viewpoint, looking towards Waterton Lake.

Above: the southern reaches of the Rocky Mountains reflected in a waterhole at Twin Buttes and *facing page* Vimy Ridge (left) and Mount Richards (right) far across Maskinonge Lake.

A fallen tree *above* on the snow-covered shoreline of Summit Lake.
From Bear's Hump Ridge may be seen the buildings of Waterton Park
townsite on the shores of Upper Waterton Lake, *facing page.*

At the entrance to Waterton Lakes is Buffalo Paddock where, against a mountainous backdrop, buffalo graze the prairie.

The waters of a stream in Red Rock Canyon, in the Blakiston Valley, flow over a multi-colored bed *left and facing page.*
    A doe mule deer grazes at Cameron Lake *top* and, *above* a lone bull bison pictured in the rutting season.

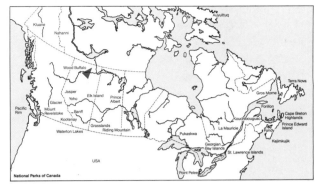

The vegetation of the Salt Plains *left* is composed of a variety of salt-resistant species. *Above:* Karst Sinkhole, near Carlson's Firetower. Sinkholes are created by surface and ground water dissolving the bedrock.

A meadow of giant dandelions *above* on a low-lying island
in Lake Claire Narrows, Peace Point, on the Athabasca
Delta. *Right:* sunset from the banks of Peace River, Peace
Point Indian Reserve.

Right: the backwash of a fishing boat foams the waters of the Peace River.
Below and facing page: willow grass reed beds at the mouth of the Mamalaw Lake.
Below right: a lone buffalo bull chewing the cud.

Wood Buffalo Park contains the largest free-roaming herd
of bison in the world. On these pages are seen only a few
of the bison that shelter within this huge park.

Autumnal dawns in the northern wilderness are spectacles
that reward the early riser. *Above,* the sun is just emerging
above the treeline, reflecting itself in the Slave River;
facing page, arrival of daylight is forecast by sluggish mist
rising from the water while the sun remains hidden.

Evening sunlight on a stand of trembling aspen *facing page*
on the banks of the Peace River, Peace Point Indian
Reserve. *Above:* **dehydrated salt mounds on the salt plains**
of Wood Buffalo Park resemble frozen patches of snow.

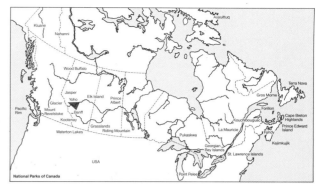

National Parks of Canada

The rail lines pass through spiral tunnels, *top left; bottom left and top right* **are two views of Mount Lefroy;** *bottom, right* **shows the barren slopes of Mount Yukness.** *Facing page:* **Schaeffer Lake, surrounded by forbidding peaks.**

The snows of autumn blanket the Mount Odaray Plateau Grand View
above and facing page.

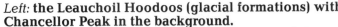

Left: the Leauchoil Hoodoos (glacial formations) with Chancellor Peak in the background.

The view *below left* is of Lefroy Lake, one of three tier lakes linking lakes O'Hara and Oesa. *Below:* O'Hara Falls with (at lower right) the emerald waters of Lake O'Hara.

Facing page: Lake Oesa, ringed by mounts Lefroy and Yukness.

Wapta Falls, *left,* **pictured at dusk from the logging road. The still waters of Emerald Lake** *above* **with, behind it, Emerald Peak (left) and Mount Carnarvon (right).**
Above right: **the lace-like beauty of Takakkaw Falls.**

Overleaf: **Photographed in Banff National Park, this Elk (or Wapiti) in early fall still sports his summer coloring.**